# Hear the Good News

A book of the Gospels for young people

## Katie Thompson

**kevin mayhew**

# kevin mayhew

First published in Great Britain in 2008 by Kevin Mayhew Ltd
Buxhall, Stowmarket, Suffolk IP14 3BW
Tel: +44 (0) 1449 737978  Fax: +44 (0) 1449 737834
E-mail: info@kevinmayhewltd.com

## www.kevinmayhew.com

© 2000 Katie Thompson

The right of Katie Thompson to be identified as the author of this work has been asserted by her in accordance with the Copyright, Designs and Patents Act 1988.

All rights reserved. No part of this publication may be reproduced, stored in a retrieval system, or transmitted, in any form or by any means, electronic, mechanical, photocopying, recording, or otherwise, without the prior written permission of the publisher.

9 8 7 6 5 4 3 2 1 OD

ISBN 978 1 84003 551 3
Catalogue No. 1500353

Cover design by Rob Mortonson
Edited by Katherine Laidler
Typesetting by Louise Selfe

Printed and bound in Great Britain

# Introduction

*'The seed sown in rich soil
is someone who hears the Word and understands it;
they will produce a rich harvest.'*
*Matthew 13:23*

This book of Gospels is a living book because it contains the living Word of God which has the power to bring about all that it proclaims. Every word spoken by Christ comes to us with the authority of God himself. Through his words and actions, Jesus reveals God's merciful love and compassion for all of humanity. If we listen to the Gospel with our hearts as well as our ears, then God can speak personally to each one of us, offering guidance and spiritual nourishment whatever our age or where we might be on our individual journey of faith. Planted in our hearts, the Word can take root and grow, so that together we can build God's kingdom in our midst by living his Gospel of love.

If the Gospel is to speak for itself, then it should be proclaimed audibly, clearly and with reverence and understanding. A reader does not communicate simply words, but an experience, where people can meet God in a very real way which can transform and enlighten their lives. With prayerful preparation, a good reader can bring the Word alive for listeners, and help them to discover the relevance of God's message in relation to their individual lives. Practical preparation for this ministry should always include careful reading of the text and practice of its delivery, and familiarisation with any difficult words. For this purpose, a guide for pronouncing biblical names can be found in the appendix at the back of this book.

For Christians everywhere, the four Gospels are at the centre of our lives. They represent the very essence of the New Testament, the heart of our faith, the Good News that Christ our Saviour is risen from the dead.

I sincerely hope that this beautiful book helps and encourages you to share that Good News with one another.

'Go out to the whole world:
proclaim the Good News to all of creation.'
*Mark 16:15*

Katie Thompson

# Contents

## YEAR A

### ADVENT

| | |
|---|---|
| First Sunday of Advent    *Matthew 24:37-44* | 15 |
| Second Sunday of Advent    *Matthew 3:1-12* | 16 |
| Third Sunday of Advent    *Matthew 11:2-11* | 17 |
| Fourth Sunday of Advent    *Matthew 1:18-24* | 18 |

### CHRISTMAS

| | |
|---|---|
| Christmas Day    *John 1:1-18* | 19 |
| The Holy Family of Jesus, Mary and Joseph    *Matthew 2:13-15, 19-23* | 20 |
| Second Sunday after Christmas    *John 1:1-18* | 21 |
| The Epiphany of the Lord    *Matthew 2:1-12* | 22 |
| The Baptism of the Lord    *Matthew 3:13-17* | 24 |

### LENT

| | |
|---|---|
| First Sunday of Lent    *Matthew 4:1-11* | 25 |
| Second Sunday of Lent    *Matthew 17:1-9* | 26 |
| Third Sunday of Lent    *John 4:5-42* | 27 |
| Fourth Sunday of Lent    *John 9:1-41* | 30 |
| Fifth Sunday of Lent    *John 11:1-45* | 32 |

### HOLY WEEK

| | |
|---|---|
| Palm (Passion) Sunday | |
|   Liturgy of the Palms    *Matthew 21:1-11* | 34 |
|   Liturgy of the Passion (longer version)    *Matthew 26:14-27:66* | 35 |
|   Liturgy of the Passion (shorter version)    *Matthew 27:11-54* | 43 |

### EASTER

| | |
|---|---|
| Easter Day    *John 20:1-9* | 46 |
| Easter Day (alternative reading)    *Matthew 28:1-10* | 47 |
| Second Sunday of Easter    *John 20:19-31* | 48 |
| Third Sunday of Easter    *Luke 24:13-35* | 50 |

CONTENTS

Fourth Sunday of Easter   *John 10:1-10*   52
Fifth Sunday of Easter   *John 14:1-12*   53
Sixth Sunday of Easter   *John 14:15-21*   54
The Ascension of the Lord   *Matthew 28:16-20*   55
Seventh Sunday of Easter   *John 17:1-11*   56
Pentecost Sunday (first reading)   *Acts 2:1-11*   57
Pentecost Sunday (Gospel)   *John 20:19-23*   58
Trinity Sunday   *John 3:16-18*   59

ORDINARY TIME

Second Sunday of the Year   *John 1:29-34*   60
Third Sunday of the Year   *Matthew 4:12-23*   61
Fourth Sunday of the Year   *Matthew 5:1-12*   62
Fifth Sunday of the Year   *Matthew 5:13-16*   63
Sixth Sunday of the Year   *Matthew 5:17-37*   64
Seventh Sunday of the Year   *Matthew 5:38-48*   66
Eighth Sunday of the Year   *Matthew 6:24-34*   67
Ninth Sunday of the Year   *Matthew 7:21-27*   68
Tenth Sunday of the Year   *Matthew 9:9-13*   69
Eleventh Sunday of the Year   *Matthew 9:36-10:8*   70
Twelfth Sunday of the Year   *Matthew 10:26-33*   71
Thirteenth Sunday of the Year   *Matthew 10:37-42*   72
Fourteenth Sunday of the Year   *Matthew 11:25-30*   73
Fifteenth Sunday of the Year   *Matthew 13:1-23*   74
Sixteenth Sunday of the Year   *Matthew 13:24-43*   76
Seventeenth Sunday of the Year   *Matthew 13:44-52*   78
Eighteenth Sunday of the Year   *Matthew 14:13-21*   80
Nineteenth Sunday of the Year   *Matthew 14:22-33*   81
Twentieth Sunday of the Year   *Matthew 15:21-28*   82
Twenty-first Sunday of the Year   *Matthew 16:13-20*   83
Twenty-second Sunday of the Year   *Matthew 16:21-27*   84
Twenty-third Sunday of the Year   *Matthew 18:15-20*   85
Twenty-fourth Sunday of the Year   *Matthew 18:21-35*   86
Twenty-fifth Sunday of the Year   *Matthew 20:1-16*   88
Twenty-sixth Sunday of the Year   *Matthew 21:28-32*   89
Twenty-seventh Sunday of the Year   *Matthew 21:33-43*   90
Twenty-eighth Sunday of the Year   *Matthew 22:1-14*   91
Twenty-ninth Sunday of the Year   *Matthew 22:15-21*   92
Thirtieth Sunday of the Year   *Matthew 22:34-40*   93
Thirty-first Sunday of the Year   *Matthew 23:1-12*   94
Thirty-second Sunday of the Year   *Matthew 25:1-13*   95

Thirty-third Sunday of the Year   *Matthew 25:14-30*   96
Christ the King   *Matthew 25:31-46*   98

# YEAR B

## ADVENT

First Sunday of Advent   *Mark 13:33-37*   103
Second Sunday of Advent   *Mark 1:1-8*   104
Third Sunday of Advent   *John 1:6-8, 19-28*   105
Fourth Sunday of Advent   *Luke 1:26-38*   106

## CHRISTMAS

Christmas Day   *Luke 2:1-14*   107
The Holy Family of Jesus, Mary and Joseph   *Luke 2:22-40*   108
Second Sunday after Christmas   *John 1:1-18*   110
The Epiphany of the Lord   *Matthew 2:1-12*   111
The Baptism of the Lord   *Mark 1:7-11*   113

## LENT

First Sunday of Lent   *Mark 1:12-15*   114
Second Sunday of Lent   *Mark 9:2-10*   115
Third Sunday of Lent   *John 2:13-25*   116
Fourth Sunday of Lent   *John 3:14-21*   117
Fifth Sunday of Lent   *John 12:20-33*   118

## HOLY WEEK

Palm (Passion) Sunday
   Liturgy of the Palms   *Mark 11:1-10*   119
   Liturgy of the Passion (longer version)   *Mark 14:1-15:47*   120
   Liturgy of the Passion (shorter version)   *Mark 15:1-39*   128

## EASTER

Easter Day   *John 20:1-9*   131
Easter Day (alternative reading)   *Mark 16:1-7*   132
Second Sunday of Easter   *John 20:19-31*   133
Third Sunday of Easter   *Luke 24:35-48*   135
Fourth Sunday of Easter   *John 10:11-18*   136
Fifth Sunday of Easter   *John 15:1-8*   137

CONTENTS

| | |
|---|---|
| Sixth Sunday of Easter   *John 15:9-17* | 138 |
| The Ascension of the Lord   *Mark 16:15-20* | 139 |
| Seventh Sunday of Easter   *John 17:11-19* | 140 |
| Pentecost Sunday (first reading)   *Acts 2:1-11* | 141 |
| Pentecost Sunday (Gospel)   *John 15:26-27; 16:12-15* | 142 |
| Trinity Sunday   *Matthew 28:16-20* | 143 |

ORDINARY TIME

| | |
|---|---|
| Second Sunday of the Year   *John 1:35-42* | 144 |
| Third Sunday of the Year   *Mark 1:14-20* | 145 |
| Fourth Sunday of the Year   *Mark 1:21-28* | 146 |
| Fifth Sunday of the Year   *Mark 1:29-39* | 147 |
| Sixth Sunday of the Year   *Mark 1:40-45* | 148 |
| Seventh Sunday of the Year   *Mark 2:1-12* | 149 |
| Eighth Sunday of the Year   *Mark 2:18-22* | 150 |
| Ninth Sunday of the Year   *Mark 2:23-3:6* | 151 |
| Tenth Sunday of the Year   *Mark 3:20-35* | 153 |
| Eleventh Sunday of the Year   *Mark 4:26-34* | 155 |
| Twelfth Sunday of the Year   *Mark 4:35-41* | 156 |
| Thirteenth Sunday of the Year   *Mark 5:21-43* | 157 |
| Fourteenth Sunday of the Year   *Mark 6:1-6* | 159 |
| Fifteenth Sunday of the Year   *Mark 6:7-13* | 160 |
| Sixteenth Sunday of the Year   *Mark 6:30-34* | 161 |
| Seventeenth Sunday of the Year   *John 6:1-15* | 162 |
| Eighteenth Sunday of the Year   *John 6:24-35* | 163 |
| Nineteenth Sunday of the Year   *John 6:41-51* | 164 |
| Twentieth Sunday of the Year   *John 6:51-58* | 165 |
| Twenty-first Sunday of the Year   *John 6:60-69* | 166 |
| Twenty-second Sunday of the Year   *Mark 7:1-8, 14-15, 21-23* | 167 |
| Twenty-third Sunday of the Year   *Mark 7:31-37* | 168 |
| Twenty-fourth Sunday of the Year   *Mark 8:27-35* | 169 |
| Twenty-fifth Sunday of the Year   *Mark 9:30-37* | 170 |
| Twenty-sixth Sunday of the Year   *Mark 9:38-43, 45, 47-48* | 171 |
| Twenty-seventh Sunday of the Year   *Mark 10:2-16* | 172 |
| Twenty-eighth Sunday of the Year   *Mark 10:17-30* | 174 |
| Twenty-ninth Sunday of the Year   *Mark 10:35-45* | 176 |
| Thirtieth Sunday of the Year   *Mark 10:46-52* | 177 |
| Thirty-first Sunday of the Year   *Mark 12:28-34* | 178 |
| Thirty-second Sunday of the Year   *Mark 12:38-44* | 179 |
| Thirty-third Sunday of the Year   *Mark 13:24-32* | 180 |
| Christ the King   *John 18:33-37* | 181 |

# YEAR C

## ADVENT

| | |
|---|---|
| First Sunday of Advent   *Luke 21:25-28, 34-36* | 185 |
| Second Sunday of Advent   *Luke 3:1-6* | 186 |
| Third Sunday of Advent   *Luke 3:10-18* | 187 |
| Fourth Sunday of Advent   *Luke 1:39-44* | 188 |

## CHRISTMAS

| | |
|---|---|
| Christmas Day   *Luke 2:15-20* | 189 |
| The Holy Family of Jesus, Mary and Joseph   *Luke 2:41-52* | 190 |
| Second Sunday after Christmas   *John 1:1-18* | 191 |
| The Epiphany of the Lord   *Matthew 2:1-12* | 192 |
| The Baptism of the Lord   *Luke 3:15-16, 21-22* | 194 |

## LENT

| | |
|---|---|
| First Sunday of Lent   *Luke 4:1-13* | 195 |
| Second Sunday of Lent   *Luke 9:28-36* | 196 |
| Third Sunday of Lent   *Luke 13:1-9* | 197 |
| Fourth Sunday of Lent   *Luke 15:1-3, 11-32* | 198 |
| Fifth Sunday of Lent   *John 8:1-11* | 200 |

## HOLY WEEK

Palm (Passion) Sunday

| | |
|---|---|
| Liturgy of the Palms   *Luke 19:28-40* | 201 |
| Liturgy of the Passion (longer version)   *Luke 22:14-23:56* | 202 |
| Liturgy of the Passion (shorter version)   *Luke 23:1-49* | 210 |

## EASTER

| | |
|---|---|
| Easter Day   *John 20:1-9* | 214 |
| Easter Day (alternative reading)   *Luke 24:1-12* | 215 |
| Second Sunday of Easter   *John 20:19-31* | 216 |
| Third Sunday of Easter   *John 21:1-19* | 218 |
| Fourth Sunday of Easter   *John 10:27-30* | 220 |
| Fifth Sunday of Easter   *John 13:31-35* | 221 |
| Sixth Sunday of Easter   *John 14:23-29* | 222 |
| The Ascension of the Lord   *Luke 24:46-53* | 223 |
| Seventh Sunday of Easter   *John 17:20-26* | 224 |
| Pentecost Sunday (first reading)   *Acts 2:1-11* | 225 |
| Pentecost Sunday (Gospel)   *John 14:15-16, 23-26* | 226 |
| Trinity Sunday   *John 16:12-15* | 227 |

CONTENTS

## ORDINARY TIME

| | | |
|---|---|---|
| Second Sunday of the Year  *John 2:1-11* | | 228 |
| Third Sunday of the Year  *Luke 1:1-4; 4:14-21* | | 229 |
| Fourth Sunday of the Year  *Luke 4:21-30* | | 230 |
| Fifth Sunday of the Year  *Luke 5:1-11* | | 231 |
| Sixth Sunday of the Year  *Luke 6:17, 20-26* | | 232 |
| Seventh Sunday of the Year  *Luke 6:27-38* | | 233 |
| Eighth Sunday of the Year  *Luke 6:39-45* | | 234 |
| Ninth Sunday of the Year  *Luke 7:1-10* | | 235 |
| Tenth Sunday of the Year  *Luke 7:11-17* | | 236 |
| Eleventh Sunday of the Year  *Luke 7:36-8:3* | | 237 |
| Twelfth Sunday of the Year  *Luke 9:18-24* | | 238 |
| Thirteenth Sunday of the Year  *Luke 9:51-62* | | 239 |
| Fourteenth Sunday of the Year  *Luke 10:1-12, 17-20* | | 240 |
| Fifteenth Sunday of the Year  *Luke 10:25-37* | | 241 |
| Sixteenth Sunday of the Year  *Luke 10:38-42* | | 243 |
| Seventeenth Sunday of the Year  *Luke 11:1-13* | | 244 |
| Eighteenth Sunday of the Year  *Luke 12:13-21* | | 245 |
| Nineteenth Sunday of the Year  *Luke 12:32-48* | | 246 |
| Twentieth Sunday of the Year  *Luke 12:49-53* | | 248 |
| Twenty-first Sunday of the Year  *Luke 13:22-30* | | 249 |
| Twenty-second Sunday of the Year  *Luke 14:1, 7-14* | | 250 |
| Twenty-third Sunday of the Year  *Luke 14:25-33* | | 251 |
| Twenty-fourth Sunday of the Year  *Luke 15:1-32* | | 252 |
| Twenty-fifth Sunday of the Year  *Luke 16:1-13* | | 254 |
| Twenty-sixth Sunday of the Year  *Luke 16:19-31* | | 256 |
| Twenty-seventh Sunday of the Year  *Luke 17:5-10* | | 257 |
| Twenty-eighth Sunday of the Year  *Luke 17:11-19* | | 258 |
| Twenty-ninth Sunday of the Year  *Luke 18:1-8* | | 259 |
| Thirtieth Sunday of the Year  *Luke 18:9-14* | | 260 |
| Thirty-first Sunday of the Year  *Luke 19:1-10* | | 261 |
| Thirty-second Sunday of the Year  *Luke 20:27-38* | | 262 |
| Thirty-third Sunday of the Year  *Luke 21:5-19* | | 263 |
| Christ the King  *Luke 23:35-43* | | 264 |

# SPECIAL FEASTS – YEARS A, B AND C

| | | |
|---|---|---|
| Mary, Mother of God – 1 January  *Luke 2:16-21* | | 267 |
| The Annunciation of the Lord – 25 March  *Luke 1:26-38* | | 268 |
| The Presentation of the Lord – 2 February  *Luke 2:22-40* | | 269 |

Saint John the Baptist – 24 June   *Luke 1:57-66, 80*   271
Saints Peter and Paul – 29 June   *Matthew 16:13-19*   272
The Transfiguration of the Lord – 6 August
    Year A – *Matthew 17:1-9*   273
    Year B – *Mark 9:2-10*   274
    Year C – *Luke 9:28-36*   275
The Assumption of the Blessed Virgin Mary – 15 August
    *Luke 1:39-56*   276
The Triumph of the Holy Cross – 14 September
    *John 3:13-17*   278
All Saints – 1 November   *Matthew 5:1-12*   279
Feasts of the Dedication of a Church   *John 4:19-24*   280


Pronunciation guide   281

# YEAR A

# First Sunday of Advent

*Matthew 24:37-44*

A reading from the Gospel of St Matthew

Jesus said to his disciples:

> Just as the flood in Noah's time took people by surprise, so too will the Son of Man come when no one expects him. You must stay alert and be ready, because you do not know when your master will return. If the owner of a house knew when the burglar planned to visit, then he would stay awake and keep guard. So you must always keep yourselves ready to welcome the Son of Man at an unexpected time.

This is the Gospel of the Lord
**Praise to you, Lord Jesus Christ**

## Second Sunday of Advent

*Matthew 3:1-12*

A reading from the Gospel of St Matthew

A man called John appeared in the Judaean desert and began to preach to the people. His coming had been foretold by the prophet Isaiah who said:

'A voice calls out in the desert,
Prepare a straight path for the Lord.'

John wore a simple camel-hair coat fastened around the middle with a leather belt, and he lived on honey and creatures living in the desert. Soon news of John spread throughout Judaea and Jordan, and people made their way to him to confess their sins and to be baptised.

When some of the Pharisees and Sadducees came to John, he gave them this warning: 'Repent and turn back to God, and do not assume that you will be saved because you are descendants of Abraham. Any tree which produces bad fruit will be cut down and burned. I baptise you with water as a sign of your repentance, but someone more powerful is coming after me, and he will baptise with the Holy Spirit. He will sort the good from the bad, and I am not worthy even to carry his sandals.'

This is the Gospel of the Lord
**Praise to you, Lord Jesus Christ**

# THIRD SUNDAY OF ADVENT

*Matthew 11:2-11*

A reading from the Gospel of St Matthew

John the Baptist had been arrested and imprisoned by King Herod, when news of Jesus and his wonderful works reached him. So John sent his friends to ask Jesus, 'Are you the promised one or is he still to come?'

Jesus said to them, 'Tell John what you have seen and heard; the blind can see, the lame can walk, the sick are cured, the deaf can hear and the dead are raised to life. The Good News of God's kingdom is being proclaimed to the poor, and blessed are those who believe in me.'

As the men left, Jesus asked the crowds gathered around him, 'Did you go to the desert expecting to see a prophet? Yes, but John is more than a prophet; he is the one of whom the Scriptures said: "I will send my messenger before you to prepare the way." No one greater than John has ever been born, and yet the least in God's kingdom is greater than he.'

This is the Gospel of the Lord
**Praise to you, Lord Jesus Christ**

# Fourth Sunday of Advent

*Matthew 1:18-24*

A reading from the Gospel of St Matthew

This is how the birth of Jesus took place. Mary, his mother, was engaged to a carpenter called Joseph; before they were married Mary told Joseph that she was expecting a child. Joseph, who was a good and kind man, wanted to protect Mary from gossip and scandal, so he decided to break off the engagement quietly.

Then one night, as he slept, an angel appeared to him and said, 'Joseph, descendant of David, do not be afraid to take Mary to be your wife. This child has been conceived by the Holy Spirit, and Mary will have a son and you must call him Jesus, for he has come to save his people from their sins.' When Joseph awoke, he did as the angel had said and took Mary to be his wife.

When the time came, she gave birth to a son and they called him Jesus. All this happened just as the Lord had promised through the prophet Isaiah when he foretold: 'See! A virgin will conceive and have a son and they will call him Emmanuel' (which means 'God is with us').

This is the Gospel of the Lord
**Praise to you, Lord Jesus Christ**

YEAR A

# CHRISTMAS DAY

*John 1:1-18*

A reading from the Gospel of St John

At the beginning of time, the Word already existed. The Word was with God; and the Word was God. From the very beginning, all things were created through him. All life came from the Word, and this life was the light for all people. The light shines out from the darkness, and the darkness could never overcome it.

God sent a man called John, to be a witness for the light, so that others would believe because of him, even though he was not the light. The real light was the Word who was coming into the world to give light to everyone.

He was in the world created through him, and yet the world did not know him. He came to his own people and they did not accept him. To those who did receive him he gave the right to become children of God, the offspring of God himself.

The Word became flesh and he lived as a man among us. We saw his glory given by the Father to his only Son, who is full of grace and truth.

John came to be his witness and he said: 'This is the one whom I spoke of when I said, "He who succeeds me, has passed before me, because he already existed." We received God's law through Moses, but it is through Jesus Christ that we receive many gifts and his grace and truth. God has never been seen, but Jesus, his only beloved son, has made God known to us as never before, because he is very close to his Father's heart.'

This is the Gospel of the Lord
**Praise to you, Lord Jesus Christ**

# THE HOLY FAMILY

*Matthew 2:13-15, 19-23*

A reading from the Gospel of St Matthew

After the wise men had left, an angel sent by God appeared to Joseph in a dream with this warning: 'Get up, Joseph! You and your family are in great danger! You must flee to Egypt this very night, and stay there until I tell you that it is safe to return. King Herod means to find Jesus and kill him!'

So Joseph got up and set off for Egypt while it was still dark. Some time later, after Herod's death, the angel returned to Joseph just as he had promised and told him that it was safe for the family to leave Egypt. So they returned once more to Galilee and made their home in a town called Nazareth.

This is the Gospel of the Lord
**Praise to you, Lord Jesus Christ**

YEAR A

# Second Sunday after Christmas

*John 1:1-18*

A reading from the Gospel of St John

At the beginning of time, the Word already existed. The Word was with God; and the Word was God. From the very beginning, all things were created through him. All life came from the Word, and this life was the light for all people. The light shines out from the darkness, and the darkness could never overcome it.

God sent a man called John, to be a witness for the light, so that others would believe because of him, even though he was not the light. The real light was the Word who was coming into the world to give light to everyone.

He was in the world created through him, and yet the world did not know him. He came to his own people and they did not accept him. To those who did receive him he gave the right to become children of God, the offspring of God himself.

The Word became flesh and he lived as a man among us. We saw his glory given by the Father to his only Son, who is full of grace and truth.

John came to be his witness and he said: 'This is the one whom I spoke of when I said, "He who succeeds me, has passed before me, because he already existed." We received God's law through Moses, but it is through Jesus Christ that we receive many gifts and his grace and truth. God has never been seen, but Jesus, his only beloved son, has made God known to us as never before, because he is very close to his Father's heart.'

This is the Gospel of the Lord
**Praise to you, Lord Jesus Christ**

# The Epiphany of the Lord

*Matthew 2:1-12*

A reading from the Gospel of St Matthew

Jesus was born in Bethlehem, a small town in Judaea when King Herod ruled the land. Some wise men from the east travelled to Jerusalem and asked King Herod where they could find the new-born King of the Jews whom they had come to worship.

Herod was greatly troubled because he didn't want anyone else to be king, so he sent for his advisers. 'Tell me where this child, the so-called King, will be born,' he said.

'It has been foretold by the prophets that he will be born in Bethlehem,' they answered.

For the prophets had written:
>   And you, Bethlehem in Judaea,
>   are not the least important among Judaean cities,
>   for from you a leader will come,
>   a shepherd for my people Israel!

King Herod sent for the wise men privately, and asked them to tell him exactly when the star had first appeared. Then he said to them, 'I will allow you to search for this child, but you must come back and tell me where to find him. Then I too can go and honour him.'

The wise men set off again on their journey. They followed the bright star until it appeared to stop over a house, where they found Mary with the baby Jesus. They were filled with wonder and joy, and, falling to their knees to worship him, they gave him gifts of gold, frankincense and myrrh.

An angel warned them in a dream not to return to Herod's palace, so they went back to their own country a different way.

This is the Gospel of the Lord
**Praise to you, Lord Jesus Christ**

# THE BAPTISM OF THE LORD

*Matthew 3:13-17*

A reading from the Gospel of St Matthew

Jesus came from Galilee to the banks of the River Jordan to be baptised by John the Baptist. John was surprised by this and said to him, 'Surely this is wrong and it should be you baptising me!'

Jesus answered, 'We will do things this way for it is right to follow my Father's plan.'

Reluctantly John agreed, and Jesus was baptised in the river. As he stood up in the water, the clouds parted and the Holy Spirit came down like a dove and settled on Jesus. Then a voice from heaven said, 'This is my Son, with whom I am very pleased.'

This is the Gospel of the Lord
**Praise to you, Lord Jesus Christ**

YEAR A

# First Sunday of Lent

*Matthew 4:1-11*

A reading from the Gospel of St Matthew

Jesus was led by the Holy Spirit into the desert where the devil came to tempt him. After fasting for forty days and nights Jesus was very hungry, and the devil said to him, 'If you are indeed the Son of God, turn the stones around you into bread.'

In reply, Jesus repeated the words of Scripture which said, 'Man cannot survive on bread alone, but needs every word spoken by God.'

Then the devil took Jesus to the Temple in Jerusalem and together they stood on its highest point. 'If you are the Son of God,' the devil said, 'then throw yourself down to prove it, because Scripture tells us that God's angels will protect you from harm.'

Again Jesus answered him with words from Scripture: 'It is not right to put God to the test.'

The devil did not give up easily, so he took Jesus to the top of a high mountain where he showed him the kingdoms of the world in all their glory. 'If you worship me,' the devil said, 'I will give all of these to you.'

Finally growing impatient, Jesus said, 'Devil, leave me alone! For Scripture tells us to worship God and serve only him.'

Finally the devil left Jesus, and angels appeared to take care of him.

This is the Gospel of the Lord
**Praise to you, Lord Jesus Christ**

# Second Sunday of Lent

*Matthew 17:1-9*

A reading from the Gospel of St Matthew

One day Jesus asked Peter, James and John to come and pray with him. He led them to the top of a steep mountain, where it was peaceful and quiet, and where they could be alone.

Jesus began to pray to his heavenly Father and suddenly he appeared to change! His face and clothes shone with a brilliant light, as dazzling as the rays of the sun.

Then the disciples saw Moses and Elijah on either side of Jesus, talking to him. Peter jumped up with excitement and said, 'Lord, this is wonderful! I could make three shelters – one for each of you!'

At that moment a cloud streaming with light appeared above them, and a voice said, 'This is my Son, whom I love very much. Listen to what he says.'

The disciples were so terrified that they threw themselves to the ground and hid their faces.

Then Jesus said gently, 'Get up, my friends, do not be afraid.'

When they looked up, Jesus was standing alone. As they came down the mountain together, Jesus told them firmly, 'You must not tell anyone about what you have seen today, until the Son of Man has risen from the dead.'

This is the Gospel of the Lord
**Praise to you, Lord Jesus Christ**

YEAR A

# Third Sunday of Lent

*John 4:5-42*

A reading from the Gospel of St John

Jesus came to a Samaritan town called Sychar and stopped to rest about midday at a place known as 'Jacob's Well'. While his disciples went into the town to buy food, Jesus waited beside the well, and before long a woman came there to draw water. When Jesus asked the woman for a drink she was taken by surprise because Jews and Samaritans rarely spoke to each other.

'Surely, sir, you are a Jew,' she said. 'So why do you ask me, a Samaritan, for a drink?'

Jesus said to her, 'If you knew me, it would be you asking me for a drink, because I would give you living water.'

The woman was puzzled and asked him, 'The well is deep and you have no bucket, so how could you reach this 'living' water?'

Jesus said, 'When you drink the water from this well, your thirst always returns. Anyone who drinks the water that I can give will never be thirsty again. This water will become a spring inside them, and fill them with eternal life.'

The woman said to him, 'Sir, share this water with me so that I never feel thirsty again.'

Jesus talked to the woman about her five previous husbands, and the man she now lived with, and he told her many things about herself that no other person knew, and she was amazed.

Then the woman said to Jesus, 'I see you are a

prophet from God, whom we Samaritans worship in our own Temple instead of the Temple in Jerusalem.'

Jesus said to her, 'It is not important where you worship, but how you worship God. Through his Spirit people will worship him in the way they should.'

The woman said to Jesus, 'I know that one day everything will be explained by the Messiah who is coming.'

Jesus said to her, 'Even now he is speaking to you. I am he.'

Just then the disciples returned, and although they were surprised to see Jesus talking to a Samaritan woman, they said nothing. Leaving her jar by the well, she ran to tell the people in the town everything the stranger had said to her, and they began to make their way to the well to meet him.

Meanwhile, the disciples encouraged Jesus to eat some of the food they had brought for him, and were puzzled when he said to them, 'I already have food which you do not know about.'

Then he explained to them, 'When I complete the work of the one who sent me, and do his will, then that is my food. You know that the harvest only begins when the crops are ready. Look around you, and see how the harvest is ready to reap. Whoever gathers in this harvest will have eternal life, and the one who sows and the one who reaps will celebrate together.'

When they heard what Jesus had told the woman at the well, many of the Samaritans believed in him. After convincing Jesus to stay in their town for a few days, the Samaritans said to each other, 'Now we have heard him for ourselves, we know that he is indeed the Saviour God promised to send.'

This is the Gospel of the Lord
**Praise to you, Lord Jesus Christ**

# Fourth Sunday of Lent

*John 9:1-41*

A reading from the Gospel of St John

One day Jesus saw a blind man begging by the roadside. The man had been blind since birth and the disciples asked Jesus, 'Master, is he blind because of sins committed by himself or his parents?'

Jesus answered, 'Neither is true! This man was born blind so that the power of God could be seen working through him. I am the light of the world, and we must do God's work while we still can.'

Then he bent down and made a paste with some spittle and a little mud. He put this on the man's eyes and said to him, 'Go to the Pool of Siloam, and wash your eyes.'

The man did this, and to his amazement found that he could see! The people of the town could not believe it. 'Is this really the blind beggar?' they asked.

Some said, 'Yes, it is', but others disagreed and said, 'No, but he resembles him.'

The crowd took the beggar to the Pharisees to tell them what had happened. The Pharisees argued amongst themselves. 'No man of God would do such a thing on the Sabbath!' some said, but others answered, 'No sinner could do such an extraordinary thing!'

Many of the people doubted that the man had really been born blind, so they sent for his parents to see what explanation they could give. 'Yes, this is our son,' they said, 'and he was born blind but now he can see. Only he can explain how this has happened, so ask him. He's old enough to answer for himself.'

So they sent for the beggar again and asked him. 'Who is this man you say cured you?'

'I do not know where he came from, or who he is, but I know that he made me see. Unless this man was sent by God he could not have done such a marvellous thing.'

The Pharisees grew angry with the man and shouted, 'Do not try to teach us when you are nothing but a sinner yourself,' and they banned him from the synagogue.

Later Jesus found him sitting alone: 'Do you believe in the Son of Man?' he asked.

'Yes, sir, I believe in him, but I do not know him,' he answered.

Jesus said, 'You can see him for he is speaking to you.'

At once, the man fell to his knees and said, 'Lord, I believe in you!'

And then Jesus said, 'I have come to make the blind see and those who can see, blind!'

'Surely you aren't implying that we are blind?' asked some of the Pharisees who were there.

Jesus said, 'You are guilty because you believe you can see already.'

This is the Gospel of the Lord
**Praise to you, Lord Jesus Christ**

# Fifth Sunday of Lent

*John 11:1-45*

A reading from the Gospel of St John

Lazarus and his two sisters, Martha and Mary, were very good friends of Jesus. They lived in a town called Bethany, not far from Jerusalem.

One day, the sisters sent an urgent message to Jesus, because Lazarus was very ill and close to death. When he heard this message, Jesus said, 'This illness will not bring death for Lazarus, but glory for God and his Son.' And he did not set off immediately, even though he was very fond of Lazarus and his sisters.

When Jesus and his disciples arrived in Bethany more than two days later, they found that Lazarus was dead, and had already been buried for four days.

Martha ran to meet Jesus and said to him, 'Lord, if you had been here, you could have saved our brother.'

Jesus said, 'Your brother will live again.'

'I know that on the last day he will come back to life,' she answered.

Jesus turned to her and said, 'I am the resurrection and the life. Anyone who believes in me will have eternal life, and he will never die. Do you believe this?'

Martha answered him, 'Yes, Lord, because I know that you are the Christ, the Son of God.'

When Jesus saw the great sadness of Martha and

Mary and their friends, he wept with love and sorrow. 'Show me where he is buried,' he said. So they took him to the tomb, where Jesus said to them, 'Roll away the stone, and you will see God's glory.'

'Lord,' Martha said, 'Lazarus has been dead for four days and by now he will smell.'

Jesus said to her, 'You will see God's glory if you believe in me.'

So they did as he said, and, looking up to heaven, Jesus prayed, 'Father, I thank you, for I know that you always listen to me. Let these people see and believe.' Then he called out in a loud voice, 'Lazarus, come out!'

To everyone's amazement Lazarus appeared, still wrapped in burial cloths, and walked from the tomb. Many people saw what happened that day, and they believed in Jesus.

This is the Gospel of the Lord
**Praise to you, Lord Jesus Christ**

# Palm (Passion) Sunday – Liturgy of the Palms

*Matthew 21:1-11*

A reading from the Gospel of St Matthew

Jesus and his disciples arrived at Bethphage on the Mount of Olives just outside Jerusalem. He sent two of the disciples to the next village to collect a donkey and her colt.

'If anyone stops you, tell them that they are for me, and will be returned,' he said.

And so it was that the prophecy was fulfilled: 'Tell Zion's daughter: see your King drawing near, humbly riding on a donkey and her colt.'

They brought the animals to Jesus, and put cloaks on their backs so that Jesus could ride on them. When the people heard that Jesus was coming they laid their cloaks on the road before him, and pulled branches off the palm trees to wave in the air. The crowds grew more and more excited, and shouted at the top of their voices, 'Hosanna, Hosanna! Blessed is the one sent by the Lord.'

Excitement filled the whole city, and some people asked, 'Who is this man?'

The people answered them, 'It is Jesus the prophet from Nazareth in Galilee.'

This is the Gospel of the Lord
**Praise to you, Lord Jesus Christ**

# Palm (Passion) Sunday – Liturgy of the Passion

*Longer version – Matthew 26:14-27:66*

A reading from the Gospel of St Matthew

The disciple called Judas, went to the chief priests to make a deal with them. 'How much will you pay me to hand Jesus over to you?' he asked.

Having agreed on a price, they sent Judas away with thirty pieces of silver, and waited for news of the betrayal he had promised.

The disciples came to Jesus on the first day of the Passover celebrations, and asked him, 'Master, where shall we prepare the Passover meal?'

Jesus sent them to find a certain man at whose house they made all the necessary preparations.

That night as Jesus shared the meal with his friends, he said to them, 'One of you is planning to betray me.'

The disciples were dismayed at his words, and one after another they asked him, 'Master, is it me?' Jesus said to them, 'My betrayer has eaten from the same dish as me tonight. Everything will happen just as the Scriptures have foretold. That man will wish he had never been born.'

Then Judas spoke up, 'Lord, surely you do not mean me!'

Looking at Judas, Jesus replied, 'You yourself have said it.'

As they were eating, Jesus took some bread and said a prayer of blessing. He broke the bread into pieces and shared it with them saying, 'Take this and eat it, this is my body.'

Then he took a cup of wine and said a prayer of thanks. He passed the cup to each of them and said, 'Take this and drink it, for this is my blood. Just as my Father promised, it will be poured out to save you from your sins. I shall not drink wine again until I do so with you in my Father's kingdom.'

Then they sang a hymn together before setting off for the Mount of Olives.

On the way there, Jesus said to them, 'Scripture tells us that the flock will scatter when their shepherd is struck down. This very night, my friends, you will all run away and desert me. But after I have risen again I will go to Galilee and wait for you there.'

Hearing this, Peter protested, 'Lord, I will never lose faith in you, even if all the others do.'

But Jesus turned to Peter and said, 'Before the cock crows at dawn, you will have denied knowing me three times.'

Peter couldn't believe what Jesus had said, and replied, 'Even if I have to die, I will never disown you,' and the other disciples agreed with everything Peter had said.

When they reached the Garden of Gethsemane, Jesus took Peter, James and John with him to pray. He was filled with great sadness and fear and said to his disciples, 'Stay awake because I need you with me tonight.' Then he began to pray, 'Father, I am afraid of what lies ahead but I will always do whatever you ask.'

When he returned to the three disciples he found

them asleep. 'Wake up!' he said. 'Could you not stay awake with me for such a short time?' Then Jesus said to Peter, 'Stay awake and pray that you will not be put to the test.'

Twice more Jesus went away and prayed as before but returned to find them all asleep again. When he returned for the third time he said to them, 'Are you still asleep? The time has arrived for the Son of Man to be handed over to sinners. Get up, my betrayer is close by. Get up, the time has come.'

Then Judas, one of the twelve disciples, appeared with a crowd of people carrying weapons, who had been sent by the chief priests and elders. Judas stepped forward and, as pre-arranged, he kissed Jesus to signal to the crowd which man they should arrest. Then they came up and seized hold of Jesus.

When the followers of Jesus realised what was happening, one of them drew his sword and angrily struck off an ear belonging to the high priest's servant. But Jesus called out to him, 'Put your sword away! If you choose to live by the sword, then you will die by it too. If I wanted to I could call down legions of angels to defend me, but everything must happen in this way if the words of Scripture are to come true!'

Then Jesus addressed the crowd and asked them, 'Why have you come to arrest me like a criminal at the dead of night, when you had so many opportunities, day after day, as I sat teaching in the Temple?' He already knew that this was to fulfil the words of Scripture.

As the crowd led Jesus away, his disciples fled into the night filled with panic and fear.

Jesus was taken before Caiaphas the High Priest and the elders. Peter followed at a distance, and waited in the palace courtyard to see what would happen next.

The accusers of Jesus were desperate to find enough evidence to have him put to death. They produced several witnesses to lie on their behalf, but still they had no proof against Jesus. One man stepped forward and told how Jesus had spoken of destroying the Temple and rebuilding it in just three days. Jesus stood silently and offered no words of defence.

Caiaphas grew increasingly frustrated and said to Jesus angrily, 'Swear by the living God to tell us truthfully whether you are indeed the Son of Man!'

Jesus replied, 'You yourself have said so, and from this time on, you will see the Son of Man sitting at his right hand and coming on the clouds of heaven.'

At these words, the whole assembly erupted in uproar and Caiaphas shouted out loud, 'We ourselves have heard this blasphemy! We have no need of any other witnesses! What is your judgement?'

Without hesitation, they answered, 'He is guilty and must be put to death,' and they began to taunt and abuse Jesus.

Meanwhile, a servant girl, who had noticed Peter sitting quietly in the high priest's courtyard, said to him, 'Weren't you with this Galilean called Jesus?' But Peter quickly denied knowing Jesus.

A short time later, when Peter was recognised again, he swore to them, 'I do not know this man called Jesus!' Some time later another member of the crowd said to Peter, 'You must be one of his disciples! You even have a Galilean accent.'

Again Peter rigorously denied knowing Jesus and he swore at them for their persistence. At that moment a cock began to crow, and, remembering what Jesus had said, Peter went away and wept.

When Judas, who had betrayed Jesus, heard that the council had sentenced him to death, he was filled with deep regret. Taking the thirty pieces of silver, he went to the chief priests and elders, and said to them, 'I have committed a terrible sin by handing over an innocent man to die.'

But they treated him with indifference because he had served their purpose. Angrily Judas threw the money at them, before running away and hanging himself. The chief priests decided to use this blood money to purchase a field to use as a graveyard, and it became known as the 'field of blood'. All this happened just as the prophet Jeremiah had foretold.

Early in the morning, Jesus was bound and taken to Pontius Pilate, the Roman governor, who had to grant permission before a sentence could be carried out.

Pilate asked Jesus, 'So is it true, are you the King of the Jews?'

'These are your words,' Jesus answered.

When the chief priests and elders began their accusations afresh, Pilate was surprised that Jesus said nothing to defend himself.

It was a custom of the time for the Roman governor to release any prisoner of the people's choice during the Passover festivities. So Pilate asked the crowd if they wanted him to release Jesus, or a well-known criminal called Barabbas. He already knew that the enemies of Jesus were driven by jealousy. Just then, a servant came to Pilate carrying a message from his wife, telling him of a dream she had dreamt warning about Jesus. 'Have nothing to do with him!' she wrote.

By this time the chief priests and elders had convinced the people to demand the release of Barabbas and the execution of Jesus. When Pilate heard them shouting, he asked in surprise, 'But what has this Jesus done wrong?'

The people shouted even louder, 'Crucify him!'

Pilate was frightened by the people's ugly mood. 'Very well,' he said, 'let the blood of this man be on your head and not mine,' and he washed his hands as a sign of his innocence.

Barabbas was released, while Jesus was whipped and then sent to be crucified.

The soldiers who led Jesus away taunted and abused him. They wrapped a scarlet cloak around him, and pressed a crown made of thorns onto his head as they shouted, 'Look at the King of the Jews now!' When they had finished jeering and making fun of him, they dressed him in his own clothes and took him away to be crucified.

As they made their way to Golgotha (the place of the skull), the soldiers forced a man called Simon, who came from Cyrene, to help Jesus to carry his cross. When they reached the place of execution, they offered Jesus a drink which he refused, and then they crucified him, and divided his clothes among themselves by throwing dice for them. Above his head they placed a sign which read 'Jesus, King of the Jews', and beside him they crucified two criminals, one on either side. They too joined in with the taunts of the crowd who had gathered to shout, 'If you could save others, why can't you save yourself'; and they jeered, 'You call yourself the Son of God, so why doesn't he rescue you now!'

At midday a blanket of darkness fell over the land for three hours, until finally Jesus cried aloud, 'My God, my God, why have you abandoned me?'

Hearing this, some onlookers believed that he was calling out to Elijah, and they watched to see if he would appear. Others went to fetch him a drink to quench his thirst, but Jesus called out once more, and then he died.

At that moment the veil which guarded the most holy place in the Temple was torn down the middle; the ground began to tremble violently, and rocks split apart; many holy people rose from the dead who would later appear in Jerusalem after the resurrection of Jesus. Seeing all this happen, the soldiers guarding Jesus were terrified and said, 'Truthfully, he was the Son of God!'

Many of the women who had followed Jesus from Galilee to care for him watched all this happen from a distance. They included Mary of Magdala; the mother of James and Joseph (also called Mary), and the mother of Zebedee's sons.

As evening fell a rich man called Joseph, who was a disciple of Jesus, arrived from Arimathaea and went to Pilate to ask for the body of Jesus. He wrapped it in a clean shroud, and laid Jesus in his own tomb which had recently been chiselled from the rock. He rolled a large stone across the entrance, watched by some of the women who sat nearby.

The chief priests and Pharisees were troubled to hear that a disciple of Jesus had taken his body away. They went to Pilate to ask for soldiers to be sent to guard the tomb where he had been laid. 'This man Jesus had talked about rising again after three days,' they said. 'His disciples could remove his body and lie about him rising from the dead. Think of how much trouble that could stir up!'

Pilate agreed with them, so the tomb was sealed and soldiers were immediately dispatched to stand guard.

This is the Gospel of the Lord
**Praise to you, Lord Jesus Christ**

YEAR A

# PALM (PASSION) SUNDAY – LITURGY OF THE PASSION

*Shorter version – Matthew 27:11-54*

A reading from the Gospel of St Matthew

Early in the morning Jesus was bound and taken to Pontius Pilate, the Roman governor, who had to grant permission before a sentence could be carried out.

Pilate asked Jesus, 'So is it true, are you the King of the Jews?'

'These are your words,' Jesus answered.

When the chief priests and elders began their accusations afresh, Pilate was surprised that Jesus said nothing to defend himself.

It was a custom of the time for the Roman governor to release any prisoner of the people's choice during the Passover festivities. So Pilate asked the crowd if they wanted him to release Jesus, or a well-known criminal called Barabbas. He already knew that the enemies of Jesus were driven by jealousy. Just then, a servant came to Pilate carrying a message from his wife, telling him of a dream she had dreamt warning about Jesus. 'Have nothing to do with him!' she wrote.

By this time, the chief priests and elders had convinced the people to demand the release of Barabbas and the execution of Jesus. When Pilate heard them shouting, he asked in surprise, 'But what has this Jesus done wrong?'

The people shouted even louder, 'Crucify him!'

Pilate was frightened by the people's ugly mood.

'Very well,' he said, 'let the blood of this man be on your head and not mine,' and he washed his hands as a sign of his innocence.

Barabbas was released, while Jesus was whipped and then sent to be crucified.

The soldiers who led Jesus away taunted and abused him. They wrapped a scarlet cloak around him, and pressed a crown made of thorns onto his head as they shouted, 'Look at the King of the Jews now!' When they had finished jeering and making fun of him, they dressed him in his own clothes and took him away to be crucified.

As they made their way to Golgotha (the place of the skull), the soldiers forced a man called Simon, who came from Cyrene, to help Jesus to carry his cross. When they reached the place of execution, they offered Jesus a drink which he refused, and then they crucified him, and divided his clothes among themselves by throwing dice for them. Above his head they placed a sign which read 'Jesus, King of the Jews', and beside him they crucified two criminals, one on either side. They too joined in with the taunts of the crowd who had gathered to shout, 'If you could save others, why can't you save yourself'; and they jeered, 'You call yourself the Son of God, so why doesn't he rescue you now!'

At midday a blanket of darkness fell over the land for three hours until finally Jesus cried aloud, 'My God, my God, why have you abandoned me?'

Hearing this, some onlookers believed that he was calling out to Elijah, and they watched to see if he would appear. Others went to fetch him a drink to quench his thirst, but Jesus called out once more, and then he died.

At that moment the veil which guarded the most holy place in the Temple was torn down the middle; the ground began to tremble violently, and rocks split apart; many holy people rose from the dead who would later appear in Jerusalem after the resurrection of Jesus. Seeing all this happen, the soldiers guarding Jesus were terrified and said, 'Truthfully, he was the Son of God!'

This is the Gospel of the Lord
**Praise to you, Lord Jesus Christ**

# Easter Day

*John 20:1-9*

A reading from the Gospel of St John

Before sunrise on the Sunday morning Mary of Magdala went to the tomb. As she reached the entrance, she saw that the stone had been rolled away and the tomb was empty. She ran to the disciples saying, 'They have taken the Lord from the tomb and we don't know where they have put him!'

Peter and another disciple, John, ran to the tomb and found it just as Mary had described, with the linen burial cloths lying on the ground. The cloth which had been wrapped around Jesus' head lay rolled up separately from the other pieces of cloth. Peter went into the tomb first, followed by John.

Until this moment they had not understood the Scriptures which had said, 'He must rise from the dead.' But now they saw, and they believed.

This is the Gospel of the Lord
**Praise to you, Lord Jesus Christ**

YEAR A

# Easter Day

*Alternative reading – Matthew 28:1-10*

A reading from the Gospel of St Matthew

At sunrise on the Sunday morning Mary of Magdala and another woman called Mary went to the tomb where Jesus was buried.

Suddenly the ground trembled violently, like an earthquake; an angel appeared, rolled the stone away from the tomb and sat on it. The angel dazzled like lightning, and the guards at the tomb were frozen with fear.

Then the angel spoke to the women, saying, 'Do not be afraid! I know that you are looking for Jesus who was crucified and buried here, but you will not find him because he is risen, just as he told you. Come and see for yourselves that he is gone! Now you must go to his disciples and tell them that he is risen, and you will see him again in Galilee. Go, and remember everything I have told you.'

Shaking with fear and excitement, the two women hurried from the tomb, and ran to tell the disciples their marvellous news. On the way Jesus suddenly appeared and greeted them with the words, 'Peace be with you!'

The women fell at his feet and worshipped the Lord.

'You have nothing to fear,' Jesus said. 'Tell my disciples to make their way to Galilee where they will see me for themselves.'

This is the Gospel of the Lord
**Praise to you, Lord Jesus Christ**

HEAR THE GOOD NEWS

## SECOND SUNDAY OF EASTER

*John 20:19-31*

A reading from the Gospel of St John

Late on the Sunday evening the disciples sat huddled together, feeling sad and afraid. The doors of the room were locked, to stop the Jews finding them.

Suddenly, Jesus appeared in the room with them and said, 'Peace be with you.'

They were amazed when they saw him and could hardly believe their eyes. But Jesus showed them the wounds in his hands and where his side had been pierced by the sword, and they were filled with joy and wonder.

Once again Jesus said, 'Peace be with you.' Then he breathed on them, saying, 'The Holy Spirit has been given to you. Whatever you choose to forgive will be forgiven. Whatever is not forgiven by you will remain unforgiven.'

The disciple called Thomas was not with the others when Jesus appeared to them. When they told him that they had seen Jesus, he scoffed at them and said, 'Unless I see for myself the wounds in his hands and his side, I will not believe you.'

Several days later, when Thomas was with the other disciples, Jesus appeared to them again, and greeted them with the words, 'Peace be with you.' Turning to Thomas he said, 'See and touch the wounds in my hands; feel the wound in my side and doubt no more.'

Thomas fell to the ground and said, 'My Lord and my God.'

Jesus said to him, 'Because you have seen you now believe, but blessed are those who have not seen and yet believe.'

Only some of the marvellous things which Jesus did and which were witnessed by his disciples are written down in this book. These have been recorded so that you might believe in Jesus, as the Christ, the Son of God, and through that faith and belief in him you may have life.

This is the Gospel of the Lord
**Praise to you, Lord Jesus Christ**

# Third Sunday of Easter

*Luke 24:13-35*

A reading from the Gospel of St Luke

On that same Sunday morning two disciples of Jesus were making their way to a village called Emmaus, a short distance from Jerusalem. They were totally miserable as they talked about the events of the past days, and the death of Jesus.

As they walked, Jesus himself joined them, but they did not recognise him.

Jesus asked them, 'What are you talking about together?'

One of them, called Cleophas, answered, 'Surely you must have heard about what happened to Jesus of Nazareth! He was a powerful prophet who was handed over to the chief priests, and the Roman governor who had him crucified. We believed that he was the Saviour sent by God. All this happened more than two days ago, and we have heard this very morning that his body is missing from the tomb where they laid him. Some of the women claimed that an angel told them that Jesus has risen and is alive, but we are not sure what has happened.'

Jesus said to them, 'Do you not believe what the prophets have foretold?' He began to explain to them the prophecies about himself in the Scriptures.

When they arrived at Emmaus, Jesus seemed to be travelling further, but because it was late in the day the disciples asked him to stay and share a meal with them.

When they were at supper Jesus took some bread, blessed it, broke it and gave it to them. At that moment they saw clearly that the stranger was in fact Jesus, but he had already disappeared from their sight.

'Of course it was the Lord,' they said. 'Remember how our hearts seemed to burn as he shared the Scriptures with us. How could we have been so blind!'

At once they returned to Jerusalem and found the other disciples gathered together and filled with joy, because Jesus had appeared to Simon.

'Yes, he is risen,' they said. 'We knew him in the breaking of the bread.' And they began to tell the others what had happened that day on the road to Emmaus.

This is the Gospel of the Lord
**Praise to you, Lord Jesus Christ**

# Fourth Sunday of Easter

*John 10:1-10*

A reading from the Gospel of St John

Jesus told the people:

> If someone enters the sheepfold by any other way than by the gate, then they are a thief and a robber. The shepherd of the sheep comes in through the gate, and the gatekeeper recognises him and lets him pass. A shepherd knows his sheep, and his sheep know him. When he calls their names, they know his voice and they follow him, one by one, through the gate of the sheepfold. The flock will not follow a stranger; instead they scatter and run away because they do not know his voice.

The people did not understand this parable, so Jesus explained to them:

> Truthfully, I am the gate, and those who came before me were thieves and robbers, and the sheep did not follow them. Anyone who enters the sheepfold through me will be saved, and they will find pasture as they go in and come out. The thief comes only to steal and destroy what is good, but I have come to give you the fullness of life.

This is the Gospel of the Lord
**Praise to you, Lord Jesus Christ**

# Fifth Sunday of Easter

*John 14:1-12*

A reading from the Gospel of St John

Jesus said to his disciples, 'Do not be afraid or worried, trust in me as you trust in God. In my Father's house there are many rooms, and I am going there to prepare a place for you. Then I shall come back to take you with me, and we will be together again. You already know the way to the place I am going.'

Thomas felt unsure and asked Jesus, 'Lord, how can we know the way if we do not know where you are going?'

Jesus answered, 'I am the way, the truth and the life. No one comes to the Father except through me, and through me you know him and have seen him already.'

Philip was troubled and he said to Jesus, 'Master, when you show us the Father, we will be content.'

'Even now you do not understand,' Jesus replied. 'Because you have seen me, you have already seen the Father. Philip, do you doubt that I am in the Father, just as he is in me? It is the Father living in me, who does his work and speaks to you. Believe what I tell you even if it is only because you have seen what I have done. Anyone who believes in me will do what I have done and more.'

This is the Gospel of the Lord
**Praise to you, Lord Jesus Christ**

# Sixth Sunday of Easter

*John 14:15-21*

A reading from the Gospel of St John

Jesus said to his disciples:

If you love me, you will obey the commandments I have given you. I will not leave you on your own; I will ask my Father to send you a helper who will stay with you always. The Spirit of God will be with you and in you, though others will not be able to see him or know that he is there. You will not be alone, and I will come back to you. Soon the world will not see me again, but you will know that I am truly alive, and, because of this, you too will truly live! Anyone who loves me follows my commandments, and my Father will love them, just as I love them, and they will come to know me.

This is the Gospel of the Lord
**Praise to you, Lord Jesus Christ**

# THE ASCENSION OF THE LORD

*Matthew 28:16-20*

A reading from the Gospel of St Matthew

The eleven apostles set off for Galilee to meet where Jesus had arranged.

When Jesus appeared before them on the mountain, several of the apostles fell to their knees and worshipped him; but some doubted.

Then he said to them, 'I have been given authority over everything in heaven and on earth, and by this authority I am sending you out to all peoples to teach them everything I have taught you. Make them my disciples and baptise them in the name of the Father, the Son and the Holy Spirit. Remember that I will never leave you; I am with you until the end of time.'

This is the Gospel of the Lord
**Praise to you, Lord Jesus Christ**

# Seventh Sunday of Easter

*John 17:1-11*

A reading from the Gospel of St John

Looking up to heaven, Jesus began to pray. 'Father, the time has come to give glory to me, so that I may glorify you. Through you, I can give eternal life to all you have placed in my care. By knowing that you are the only, true God, and I am the Christ sent by you, eternal life is theirs.'

Then Jesus said, 'Father, I have glorified you on earth by finishing the work you gave me to do; now glorify me in your heavenly presence. I have told my disciples all about you, and they know that you sent me here, and that through your power I have been able to do many wonderful things. They have listened to me teaching and they truly believe in you. Holy Father, I pray that you will keep them safe when I have gone, so that they may be one as you and I are one.'

This is the Gospel of the Lord
**Praise to you, Lord Jesus Christ**

# PENTECOST SUNDAY

*First reading – Acts 2:1-11*

A reading from the Acts of the Apostles

The disciples had gathered together in Jerusalem to celebrate the Feast of Pentecost and to wait for the Holy Spirit that Jesus had promised to send.

One day, as they were praying together, the room was suddenly filled with the sound of a powerful wind which roared through the house. Then, what looked like small tongues of fire appeared and spread out to touch each one of them. So it was that they were filled with the Holy Spirit.

At once, in their excitement, they rushed outside to tell everyone what had happened to them. As they began to speak, they were amazed to find that everyone listening to their words could understand them! People from different regions and countries were astounded to hear these men preaching to them in their own native languages.

This is the Word of the Lord
**Thanks be to God**

# Pentecost Sunday

*Gospel – John 20:19-23*

A reading from the Gospel of St John

Late in the evening the disciples sat huddled together, feeling sad and afraid. The doors of the room were locked, to stop the Jews finding them.

Suddenly, Jesus appeared in the room with them and said, 'Peace be with you.'

They were amazed when they saw him and could hardly believe their eyes. But Jesus showed them the wounds in his hands and where his side had been pierced by the sword. They were filled with joy and wonder.

Jesus said to them, 'Peace be with you. Just as my Father sent me, so I am sending you.'

Then he breathed on them, saying, 'The Holy Spirit has been given to you. Whatever you choose to forgive will be forgiven. Whatever is not forgiven by you will remain unforgiven.'

This is the Gospel of the Lord
**Praise to you, Lord Jesus Christ**

# Trinity Sunday

*John 3:16-18*

A reading from the Gospel of St John

God loved the world so much that he sent his only Son to save all who believe in him, so that they may have eternal life. He comes as a Saviour for the world and not as a judge. Those who believe will not be judged, but anyone who does not believe in the only Son of God has already passed judgement on themselves.

This is the Gospel of the Lord
**Praise to you, Lord Jesus Christ**

## SECOND SUNDAY OF THE YEAR

*John 1:29-34*

A reading from the Gospel of St John

When John saw Jesus in the distance walking towards him, he said to the crowds, 'Look, there is Jesus, the Lamb of God. He is the special one sent by God and whom I have told you about. I came to baptise you with water so that you might come to know him. I saw the Holy Spirit, hovering like a dove, coming down from heaven and settling on him, and by this sign God revealed him to me. He is the one you must follow now, for he will baptise you with the Holy Spirit.'

This is the Gospel of the Lord
**Praise to you, Lord Jesus Christ**

# Third Sunday of the Year

*Matthew 4:12-23*

A reading from the Gospel of St Matthew

When Jesus heard that John the Baptist had been arrested, he went to live in Capernaum, a fishing village beside the Sea of Galilee. All this happened just as the prophet Isaiah had foretold.

Jesus began preaching to the people and calling them to turn away from sin, because the kingdom of heaven was near.

One day, as he was walking by the Sea of Galilee, he saw two brothers out fishing together. Their names were Simon Peter and Andrew. Jesus spoke to them and said, 'Come and follow me, and I will make you fishers of people.'

The two brothers left their boat and nets at once, and followed him.

A little further on Jesus saw James and John, mending nets with their father, Zebedee. Again, Jesus asked them to follow him, and they left their father and went with him.

Jesus travelled throughout Galilee, preaching in the synagogues and proclaiming the Good News of the kingdom, and he cured many of the sick who came to him.

This is the Gospel of the Lord
**Praise to you, Lord Jesus Christ**

# Fourth Sunday of the Year

*Matthew 5:1-12*

A reading from the Gospel of St Matthew

A crowd of disciples gathered around, and Jesus sat down and began to preach to them:

Happy are the poor in spirit, for the kingdom of heaven is theirs.

Happy are the broken-hearted, for they will be comforted.

Happy are the meek and gentle, for the earth will belong to them.

Happy are those who hunger and thirst for what is right, for justice will be theirs.

Happy are those who show forgiveness, because they will receive forgiveness in return.

Happy are those with a pure heart, for they shall see the face of God.

Happy are the peace-makers; God will call them his children.

Happy are those who suffer because they stand up for what is right; the kingdom of heaven belongs to them.

Be happy when people harass and mistreat you, and tell lies about you because you are my disciples. All this was suffered by the prophets who came before you. Be glad because when the time comes you will be richly rewarded in heaven.

This is the Gospel of the Lord
**Praise to you, Lord Jesus Christ**

# Fifth Sunday of the Year

*Matthew 5:13-16*

A reading from the Gospel of St Matthew

Jesus said:

> You are like salt for the world, but if salt becomes tasteless how can it be made salty again? It is useless without its saltiness, so people throw it away. You are like a light shining for the whole world to see; just as a city built high on a hill cannot be hidden from view. No one lights a lamp and then covers it up with a bowl; they put it high up on a stand so that it gives light to everyone in the house. When you are good you will bring light into the world around you, and others will see you and thank God for sharing his goodness.

This is the Gospel of the Lord
**Praise to you, Lord Jesus Christ**

# SIXTH SUNDAY OF THE YEAR

*Matthew 5:17-37*

A reading from the Gospel of St Matthew

Jesus said:

I have not come to do away with the law or the prophets, but to make them complete. The law will remain unchanged until the end of time when it will be fulfilled. So anyone who disobeys the commandments and encourages others to do likewise will rank least in the kingdom of heaven. Those who keep God's commandments and lead others to do the same, will be considered truly great.

Listen to me. Unless your goodness is greater than that of the scribes and the Pharisees, you will never make your way into the kingdom of heaven.

In the past, if someone took a person's life they were called before the court to answer for their wickedness. I tell you now that any one who loses their temper in anger, or calls someone 'fool' or 'traitor', will be called to answer for those actions too. So if you come before God to offer your gift to him, and then remember that you have upset someone or given them cause to complain about you, go away and make your peace with them first.

If someone has an argument or dispute with you, settle that disagreement early before you end up in court and are punished.

You already know that it is wrong to break your marriage promises, but I tell you now that it is wrong even to want someone else's husband or wife to be your own. It is better to lose a part of your body which causes you to sin than have the whole body punished in hell.

In the past, a man could give his wife a written notice of divorce; but I tell you now, if he divorces her for any reason other than her being unfaithful to their marriage promises, then she will become an adulteress if she remarries, and her new partner will be guilty of adultery too.

Now I tell you, when you make a promise, do not swear by heaven, since heaven is God's throne; do not swear by earth, since that is God's footstool; nor by Jerusalem for that is the great King's holy city.

Do not even swear by the hairs on your head, since you cannot turn even a single hair black or white. All you need to say is simply 'yes' or 'no'; and nothing more.

This is the Gospel of the Lord
**Praise to you, Lord Jesus Christ**

# Seventh Sunday of the Year

*Matthew 5:38-48*

A reading from the Gospel of St Matthew

Jesus said:

In the past you have heard, 'take an eye for an eye and a tooth for a tooth'. Now I tell you, do not take revenge against someone who has wronged you; if someone hits you, do not hit them back. When you are told to do something, do more than you are asked. When someone asks for something, give it to them, and lend to those who need to borrow from you.

In the past you have learned to 'love you friends and hate your enemies'. But now I tell you that you must love your enemies and pray for anyone who wishes you harm. It is easy to love someone who loves you back, but it is hard to love someone who hurts you. Even the tax collectors and Gentiles love those who love them in return. You must try to become perfect like your heavenly Father.

This is the Gospel of the Lord
**Praise to you, Lord Jesus Christ**

# Eighth Sunday of the Year

*Matthew 6:24-34*

A reading from the Gospel of St Matthew

One day Jesus said to his friends:

You cannot have two masters because you will always prefer one to the other. In the same way, you cannot have both God and money as your masters.

Do not worry about what you have to eat and to drink, or how to clothe yourselves. Life is more important than food, and the body is more important than the clothes you cover it with. Look at the wild birds around you; they do not plant seeds to harvest and store, yet your heavenly Father feeds them. Surely your lives are more precious than those of the birds. See the wild flowers in the field; they do not clothe themselves, and yet they are more beautifully dressed than even King Solomon himself! God dresses all these flowers, and yet how unimportant they are compared to you! So do not worry about what tomorrow holds, because God will take care of all your needs. Live a life filled with goodness and do as my Father commands, and he will take care of all your worries.

This is the Gospel of the Lord
**Praise to you, Lord Jesus Christ**

# NINTH SUNDAY OF THE YEAR

*Matthew 7:21-27*

A reading from the Gospel of St Matthew

Jesus said:

> Do not assume that by calling me 'Lord, Lord' you will have a place in the kingdom of heaven. Only those who do my Father's will can expect to have a place there. At the end of time many will cry out, 'Lord, did we not do your will!' But I will not know them and I will send them away!
>
> Whoever listens to me and obeys my words is like a wise man who built his house on rock. The wind howled, the rain poured down and the rivers burst their banks and flooded the land. The house built on rock stood firm and did not fall. But whoever listens to me and disobeys my words is like a foolish man who built his house on sand. The wind howled, and the rain poured down and the rivers burst their banks and flooded the land. The house collapsed and fell because it was built on sand.

This is the Gospel of the Lord
**Praise to you, Lord Jesus Christ**

# Tenth Sunday of the Year

*Matthew 9:9-13*

A reading from the Gospel of St Matthew.

One day as Jesus was walking along he saw a man called Matthew who was a tax collector. He went over to him and said, 'Follow me.'

Matthew did as Jesus told him, and they went to Matthew's house where Jesus stayed for a meal. Many other tax collectors came and shared the meal with Jesus and his disciples.

Some Pharisees asked the disciples, 'Why is your master friendly with such dishonest sinners?'

When Jesus heard this he said to the Pharisees, 'It is sick people who need to see a doctor, not those who are healthy and well! I have not come to call the virtuous and good to follow me, but people such as these tax collectors.'

This is the Gospel of the Lord
**Praise to you, Lord Jesus Christ**

# Eleventh Sunday of the Year

*Matthew 9:36-10:8*

A reading from the Gospel of St Matthew

When Jesus saw how many people needed his help, he felt sorry for them, for they were like a flock without a shepherd to care for them. 'The harvest is rich,' he told his disciples, 'but there are few to gather it in, so we must ask the Lord to send out more labourers.'

Then Jesus called together twelve of his disciples, and gave them the power to work in his name, before sending them out all over the land to heal the sick and preach to the people. The names of the twelve were: Simon, whom Jesus called Peter, and his brother Andrew; James and his brother John, the sons of Zebedee; Philip and Bartholomew; Matthew and Thomas; James the son of Alphaeus, and Thaddaeus; Simon the zealot, and Judas Iscariot who would later betray Jesus.

Jesus said to the chosen twelve, 'Do not go to the Gentiles or the Samaritans, but go to the lost sheep of Israel, and tell them that the kingdom of heaven is very near. Cure those who are ill, raise the dead to life and cast out demons. Freely give what you have received to everyone you meet.'

This is the Gospel of the Lord
**Praise to you, Lord Jesus Christ**

YEAR A

# Twelfth Sunday of the Year

*Matthew 10:26-33*

A reading from the Gospel of St Matthew

Jesus said:

> Do not be afraid. What is concealed will be revealed, and everything will become clear to you. What I tell you at night, you will tell in broad daylight; what is spoken in whispers, you will shout from the rooftops. Do not fear those who can do you physical harm, but the one who can destroy your body and soul.

> My heavenly Father knows when even one little sparrow falls dead from the sky, and you mean more to him than all the birds in the world. He even knows the number of hairs growing on your head! If you stand up in public on my behalf, then I shall stand up on your behalf before my heavenly Father. But anyone who denies me will in turn be denied.

This is the Gospel of the Lord
**Praise to you, Lord Jesus Christ**

## THIRTEENTH SUNDAY OF THE YEAR

*Matthew 10:37-42*

A reading from the Gospel of St Matthew

Jesus said to his disciples:

It is not easy to be a disciple of mine and to follow me. Many will argue and disagree with you, and even your own family may turn away. Anyone who suffers such things as these for my sake will gain everlasting life. Anyone who welcomes you welcomes me, and in this way they welcome my heavenly Father too. Anyone who welcomes one of God's servants will share in that servant's reward. Anyone who gives even a cup of cold water to one of the least of my disciples will certainly be rewarded.

This is the Gospel of the Lord
**Praise to you, Lord Jesus Christ**

# Fourteenth Sunday of the Year

*Matthew 11:25-30*

A reading from the Gospel of St Matthew

Jesus said:

> Praise be to you, Father, for you have not chosen to reveal yourself to the clever and wise, but to unknowing children. Everything I have has been given to me by my Father; only he knows the Son, as only the Son, and those to whom I have revealed him, know the Father. Come to me, all of you who are weary of your heavy loads, and I will give you rest. Take my yoke on your shoulders, and learn from me, and you will find relief. The yoke I give you to carry is easy, and the load I give you is light.

This is the Gospel of the Lord
**Praise to you, Lord Jesus Christ**

# Fifteenth Sunday of the Year

*Matthew 13:1-23*

A reading from the Gospel of St Matthew

A crowd had gathered to listen to Jesus, and because there were so many, Jesus preached to them from a boat. He began to teach them, using parables to help them to understand his message:

> One day a farmer went out to sow some seeds in his field. As he scattered the seeds some fell on the stony path at the edge of the field, where flocks of hungry birds flew down and gobbled them up. Some seeds fell on rocky ground where, although they sprouted, the soil was too shallow for their roots, and the baking hot sun shrivelled them up. Other seeds fell where weeds were growing, and the weeds choked them until they died. Some of the seeds landed on the farmer's richest soil, and grew into strong and healthy plants.

The disciples asked Jesus why he used parables to teach the people. Jesus answered, 'Even though they have eyes to look, they cannot see; and ears to listen with, they cannot hear. Just as the prophet Isaiah said:

> The people will listen but will not understand.
> They will look but will not see clearly.
> Their hearts are hardened.
> Their hearing is dulled
> and their eyes are tightly closed.
> They do not understand
> how to change and be healed.

'You have been blessed with eyes that see and ears

that listen and understand. The kingdom of heaven is revealed to you, and many have yearned to witness what you are witnessing today!'

Then Jesus explained the meaning of this story to the people:

> The seeds are the things which I teach you, the Good News about God's kingdom. Some people hear God's word but they do not understand. This is the seed which falls on the stony path. Some people welcome my words and try hard to follow my ways at first, but when trouble or persecution comes, then they give up. They are like the seeds which fall on rocky ground; they sprout but then shrivel and die. Some people hear my message, but their hearts are filled with the cares of the world and their longing for riches. The message becomes choked like the seeds choked with weeds, and they cannot produce fruit. The seed that falls on rich soil is like those who hear my message and understand it; they bear much fruit.

This is the Gospel of the Lord
**Praise to you, Lord Jesus Christ**

# Sixteenth Sunday of the Year

*Matthew 13:24-43*

A reading from the Gospel of St Matthew

Jesus told the people a parable:

> One day a farmer sowed his field with wheat, but that night, as he slept, his enemy crept into the field and scattered weed seeds amongst the wheat. Days passed and as the wheat sprouted and grew, so did the weeds, and the farmer realised what his enemy had done. One of the farm workers asked him, 'Master, do you want us to pull up the weeds?' But the farmer answered, 'No, let them grow together until harvest time, because if you pull up the weeds now you might pull up the wheat too! When the harvest comes, the harvesters can separate the wheat from the weeds. Then I can store the wheat in my barn, and burn the weeds.'

Then Jesus told more parables about the kingdom of heaven. In the first, he said:

> God's kingdom is like a tiny mustard seed. Night and day, the little seed sprouts and grows, until one day it has become a large and leafy shrub, and the birds of the air find shelter in its many branches.

Then he told them another parable, saying, 'Imagine a woman baking bread. She takes a small amount of yeast, mixes it with flour, and before long, the dough rises and increases in size.'

Later the disciples asked Jesus to explain the story about the farmer sowing his seed, and he said to them:

I am the man who sowed the wheat, and the devil is my enemy who scattered the weeds. The wheat seeds are the people who hear my word and follow me, and the weeds are the wicked people who will not listen to me. The end of the world will be like harvest time, when good and bad people will be separated by angels sent by God. The good people will share God's glory and happiness in heaven, but the wicked people will be punished and will never see God.

The virtuous and good will shine as radiantly as the sun in the kingdom of God. If you have ears to hear with, then listen well to what I am telling you!

This is the Gospel of the Lord
**Praise to you, Lord Jesus Christ**

# Seventeenth Sunday of the Year

*Matthew 13:44-52*

A reading from the Gospel of St Matthew

Jesus compared the kingdom of heaven to priceless treasure as he said:

One day a man was digging in a field when his spade struck a box which was buried there. When he opened the box he was amazed to find it was full of treasure. He quickly buried the treasure again, went away and sold his house and all that he owned. With the money he made, he bought the field from the farmer, and then ran back and dug up the treasure. There was another man who was a merchant who bought and sold pearls to earn a living. One day he happened to find the most perfect, beautiful pearl he had ever seen. He too went away and sold everything so that he would have enough money to buy that pearl for himself.

Just as a fisherman's net is filled with many different kinds of fish, so the kingdom of heaven is filled with many different kinds of people. The fisherman sorts through his catch, keeping the good fish and throwing the worthless ones away. In the same way, good and bad people will be separated at the end of time and the worthless ones will be destroyed.

Then Jesus asked them, 'Do you understand what I have said?'

'Yes,' they replied.

And Jesus said to them, 'This means that every teacher or scribe who becomes a disciple in God's kingdom is like someone who owns a house and takes new things as well as old things out of his store cupboard.'

This is the Gospel of the Lord
**Praise to you, Lord Jesus Christ**

# Eighteenth Sunday of the Year

*Matthew 14:13-21*

A reading from the Gospel of St Matthew

A large crowd had followed Jesus to a deserted place beside the Sea of Galilee, to hear his teaching and to bring those who were sick to be healed. As it grew late in the day the disciples asked Jesus to send the people away to find some food for themselves.

'They do not need to leave,' said Jesus. 'You can give them something to eat.'

'But all we have for ourselves are five loaves and two fish!' exclaimed the disciples.

'Bring the food to me,' said Jesus and he told the crowds to sit down quietly.

Jesus took the loaves and fish and gave thanks to God. He blessed the bread, broke it, and handed it to the disciples to share with the people. There was plenty for everyone to eat, and when they had finished eating, they filled twelve baskets with the scraps. Not including the women and children, Jesus fed about five thousand people that day.

This is the Gospel of the Lord
**Praise to you, Lord Jesus Christ**

# NINETEENTH SUNDAY OF THE YEAR

*Matthew 14:22-33*

A reading from the Gospel of St Matthew

Jesus told his disciples to sail to the other side of the lake. Then he sent the crowds away and went up into the hills to pray alone. As night fell, the wind grew stronger and the disciples' boat was tossed about by the waves. In the darkness, just before dawn, Jesus came to them, walking on the water, and they were terrified because they thought it was a ghost! But Jesus called to them, 'Don't be afraid, it's me!'

Peter shouted to Jesus, 'Lord, if that really is you, tell me to come to you across the water.'

'Come!' said Jesus.

So Peter climbed out of the boat and lowered himself on to the water. Looking straight at Jesus, he began to walk towards him, but as he moved further from the boat and felt the strength of the wind, he grew afraid. Suddenly he began to sink and he cried out, 'Save me, Lord!'

As Jesus reached out his hand and pulled Peter to safety he said, 'Why did you not trust me, Peter? Is your faith so weak?'

When they got back into the boat, the wind dropped and the other disciples knelt before Jesus and said, 'You are truly the Son of God.'

This is the Gospel of the Lord
**Praise to you, Lord Jesus Christ**

HEAR THE GOOD NEWS

# TWENTIETH SUNDAY OF THE YEAR

*Matthew 15:21-28*

A reading from the Gospel of St Matthew

Jesus went to stay near the cities of Tyre and Sidon, where few people knew him. One day a Canaanite woman came to him and cried, 'Help me, Lord! My daughter's mind is disturbed and she is very ill!'

Jesus did not answer the woman, and she carried on crying aloud and begging him to help. The disciples were embarrassed by the shouting and asked Jesus to send her away.

Then Jesus said, 'I have been sent to the Jewish people and not the pagans.'

But the woman knelt at his feet and said, 'Lord, help me.'

'Surely you would not take the food meant for children and give it to the dog?' Jesus asked.

The woman answered, 'No, sir, but even dogs get the crumbs that their masters drop from the table!'

Then Jesus smiled and said, 'Your faith is strong, and your daughter is well!'

From that moment the woman's daughter was cured.

This is the Gospel of the Lord
**Praise to you, Lord Jesus Christ**

# Twenty-first Sunday of the Year

*Matthew 16:13-20*

A reading from the Gospel of St Matthew

One day Jesus asked his disciples, 'Who do people say that I am?'

'Some people say that you are John the Baptist; others say that you are Elijah or Jeremiah or one of the other wise prophets from the past.'

Then Jesus said, 'But who do you say that I am?'

The disciples were silent until Peter said, 'You are the Christ, the Son of the living God.'

Jesus smiled at Peter and said, 'My heavenly Father has helped you to understand this. You are Peter (Petros), and on this rock (Petra) I will build my Church. I will give you the keys to the kingdom of heaven; whatever you enforce here on earth will be enforced in heaven, whatever you dismiss here on earth will be dismissed in heaven.'

Then Jesus ordered his disciples not to tell anyone that he was the Christ, the Messiah that God had promised.

This is the Gospel of the Lord
**Praise to you, Lord Jesus Christ**

# Twenty-second Sunday of the Year

*Matthew 16:21-27*

A reading from the Gospel of St Matthew

Jesus began to tell his disciples that he would be brought before the high priests in Jerusalem, and would be put to death before rising to life again.

'Lord, this cannot be allowed to happen!' exclaimed Peter, who was deeply upset by what Jesus had told them.

But Jesus said, 'Peter, you are standing in my way, and your way is not God's way.'

Then Jesus told his disciples:

> If anyone wants to follow me, then they must take up their cross and put their own needs aside. Anyone who gives up their life for me will truly live. How can it be worth having the world if it means giving up life itself? Once life is lost, then it has gone for ever! When the Son of Man comes in glory, he will reward each of you according to your actions.

This is the Gospel of the Lord
**Praise to you, Lord Jesus Christ**

# Twenty-third Sunday of the Year

*Matthew 18:15-20*

A reading from the Gospel of St Matthew

Jesus said to his disciples:

> If your brother does something wrong, then go and see him and try to sort it out quietly, between yourselves. Hopefully he will listen to you, and everything will be put right. If he will not listen to you, do not give up! Take some others with you and see if he will listen to them instead. Do everything you can to win your brother back. If he still refuses to listen to the arguments and advice of others, then deal with him as you would a Gentile or a tax collector.
>
> Listen to me: whatever you accept on earth will be accepted in heaven, and whatever you forbid on earth will be forbidden in heaven. When two of you agree to ask for something, then my Father will answer your prayers. Again I tell you that when two or three of you meet together in my name, then I will be there with you.

This is the Gospel of the Lord
**Praise to you, Lord Jesus Christ**

# TWENTY-FOURTH SUNDAY OF THE YEAR

*Matthew 18:21-35*

A reading from the Gospel of St Matthew

Peter came to Jesus and asked him, 'How many times must I forgive someone who does me wrong, Lord? Should it be as many as seven times?'

Jesus answered, 'Not just seven times Peter, but as many as seventy-seven times!'

Then Jesus told a parable about the kingdom of heaven.

> There was once a king who had many servants. One servant owed the king a great deal of money, but he had nothing to pay him with. 'I will sell you and your family as slaves, and use the money to pay for your debts,' said the king.
>
> The servant fell to his knees and begged for another chance. 'Somehow I will repay everything I owe,' he pleaded. The king was a kind and generous man and, taking pity on the servant, cancelled his debts and let him go.
>
> Later that day, the same servant met another man who owed him a small amount of money. When he could not pay what he owed, the servant had him thrown into jail.
>
> When the news reached the king, he sent for the unforgiving servant. 'Could you not forgive someone just as I forgave you?' he asked. Then he had the servant thrown into prison until he could pay back all that he owed the king.

Jesus said, 'This is how my heavenly Father will treat you unless you forgive others with all your heart.'

This is the Gospel of the Lord
**Praise to you, Lord Jesus Christ**

# Twenty-fifth Sunday of the Year

*Matthew 20:1-16*

A reading from the Gospel of St Matthew

Jesus told his disciples this parable about the kingdom of heaven.

> Early one morning the owner of a vineyard went to hire some men to work for him. He agreed to pay each of them one pound per day. The landowner went out again at nine o'clock, midday and three o'clock and hired some more men to work in his vineyard, promising to pay them whatever was fair. Finally, at five o'clock, he went out and found others waiting for work and sent them to his vineyard as well.
>
> At the end of the day he paid all of the workers one pound each, even those who had not started work until five o'clock. So those who had been hired first began to grumble. 'Why have you paid these men the same as us, when we have worked all day in the hot sun, and they have only worked for an hour?' they said.
>
> The owner of the vineyard answered, 'We agreed that you would be paid one pound per day, and I have been fair. I can choose how to spend my money, so don't complain because I have been generous.'

'In this way,' Jesus said, 'those who are last will be first, and the first will be last.'

This is the Gospel of the Lord
**Praise to you, Lord Jesus Christ**

# Twenty-sixth Sunday of the Year

*Matthew 21:28-32*

A reading from the Gospel of St Matthew

Jesus told this story to the high priests.

> Once there was a man who had two sons. He said to the older one, 'Go and work in the vineyard today.'
>
> But the son answered, 'I will not go because I don't want to.' Later the son changed his mind and went to work after all.
>
> When the man asked his other son to go and work in his vineyard too, he said, 'Of course I will go,' but he did not do what he said he would.

Jesus asked the high priests, 'Which of these sons did what their father wanted?'

'The older one, of course,' they replied.

Jesus said to them, 'The people you call sinners will enter God's kingdom before any of you, because they listened and believed what John the Baptist told them. Even when you witnessed that, you did not change your minds and believe him.'

This is the Gospel of the Lord
**Praise to you, Lord Jesus Christ**

# TWENTY-SEVENTH SUNDAY OF THE YEAR

*Matthew 21:33-43*

A reading from the Gospel of St Matthew

Jesus told another parable to the people.

There was once a farmer who owned a vineyard. He had to go away on business, and so he put some farm workers in charge of the vineyard. When it was time to harvest the grapes, the farmer sent some servants to collect his share. But the farm workers beat his servants and chased them away. The farmer did not give up, and sent more servants to collect what belonged to him. Again, they were beaten and chased off.

Finally the farmer sent his own son. 'I am sure that they will treat him better,' he said.

Instead the farm workers seized the son and killed him.

Then Jesus asked, 'What will the farmer do when he arrives at the vineyard?'

The people who had been listening answered, 'He will punish the farm workers and put other people in charge of his vineyard.'

Then Jesus said to them, 'Do you remember the words of Scripture? "The stone which the builders discarded has become the most important stone of all. This is God's doing and we marvel at his work." Listen to me! God's kingdom will be taken from you and given to other people who will bear fruit!'

This is the Gospel of the Lord
**Praise to you, Lord Jesus Christ**

# Twenty-eighth Sunday of the Year

*Matthew 22:1-14*

A reading from the Gospel of St Matthew

One day Jesus told this parable about the kingdom of heaven.

A king planned a great party for his son's wedding. When everything was ready, he sent his servants to tell all the guests who had been invited to come and join in the celebrations, but each of them had an excuse for not coming.

The king was furious and said to his servants, 'These people do not deserve to share in my party, so go out and invite everyone you meet; they can come to the wedding instead!'

Soon the hall was filled with people, good and bad alike. The king noticed one man who had not bothered to dress for the occasion. He sent for his servants and the man was thrown out into the dark.

Then Jesus said, 'Many people are invited, but few are chosen.'

This is the Gospel of the Lord
**Praise to you, Lord Jesus Christ**

# Twenty-ninth Sunday of the Year

*Matthew 22:15-21*

A reading from the Gospel of St Matthew

The Pharisees wanted to trick Jesus into saying something which would get him into trouble. So they went to him and said, 'We know that you are honest and are not afraid to speak the truth. Tell us then, should we pay taxes to Caesar or not?'

Jesus answered, 'Why do you want to trick me? Show me your money.'

They gave him a Roman denarius and he asked them, 'Who is the person on this coin?'

'Caesar,' they answered.

Then Jesus said, 'Pay Caesar what belongs to him, and pay to God what belongs to God.'

This is the Gospel of the Lord
**Praise to you, Lord Jesus Christ**

# Thirtieth Sunday of the Year

*Matthew 22:34-40*

A reading from the Gospel of St Matthew

Again the Pharisees asked Jesus a question which was meant to trick him. 'Which of the commandments is the greatest?' they asked.

Jesus answered, 'You must love the Lord your God with all your heart, and all your soul and with all your mind; this is the first and most important commandment. The second greatest commandment is: you must love your neighbour as yourself. All the other rules are based on these two commandments.'

This is the Gospel of the Lord
**Praise to you, Lord Jesus Christ**

# THIRTY-FIRST SUNDAY OF THE YEAR

*Matthew 23:1-12*

A reading from the Gospel of St Matthew

Jesus spoke to his disciples and the crowd that had gathered to listen to him.

> The scribes and Pharisees hand on the teachings of Moses, so you should listen to what they tell you; however, do not be guided by what they do, since they do not practise what they preach. Their grand gestures and fussy obedience of the law serve to draw attention to themselves. Even the large bands they wear on their heads or arms, and the long tassels hanging from their cloaks emphasise their goodness for all to see. They take pride and delight in taking the place of honour and being admired by others who call them 'teacher'. You, however, are not to follow their example. You are all brothers with only one master, and one Father who is in heaven. No one is your teacher, except the Christ, so let no one call you 'teacher'. Each of you must be ready to serve the others, however great you are, because the humble will be raised up, and the self-important will be humbled.

This is the Gospel of the Lord
**Praise to you, Lord Jesus Christ**

# THIRTY-SECOND SUNDAY OF THE YEAR

*Matthew 25:1-13*

A reading from the Gospel of St Matthew

Jesus told a parable about the kingdom of heaven.

Ten bridesmaids were getting ready for a wedding, and together they went to greet the bridegroom, although they were not sure when he would come, or how long they would have to wait.

Five of them were sensible girls who brought flasks of oil to refill their lamps; the other girls did not. The bridegroom was late, and after waiting all afternoon and all evening, the bridesmaids finally fell asleep.

It was already midnight when somebody cried, 'The bridegroom is coming! Quickly go and greet him!'

The wise bridesmaids refilled their lamps and went to meet him, but the lamps of the foolish girls had gone out, and they had to go off to buy more oil. When they returned, the bridegroom and the five bridesmaids had already gone into the wedding hall.

When they knocked on the door and asked to be let in, the bridegroom sent them away saying, 'Leave here, because I do not know you!'

Then Jesus said, 'So keep watch and stay alert, for no one knows the day or time.'

This is the Gospel of the Lord
**Praise to you, Lord Jesus Christ**

# Thirty-third Sunday of the Year

*Matthew 25:14-30*

A reading from the Gospel of St Matthew

Jesus told the people a parable.

The master of a household was going abroad for some time, so he called for his servants and said to them, 'I am splitting my property between you according to your skill for managing it.'

He gave each man a number of talents which were large amounts of money. To the first he gave five talents, to the second he gave two and the third man received one. The first two men used their talents wisely, and soon doubled the amount they had been given. The man who received only one talent hid it away out of sight.

A long time later, the master of the house returned from his travels and called for his servants to see how they had invested his money. The first two servants stepped forward and presented him with double the amount they have been given.

'Well done,' the master said. 'Now I know that you can be trusted with small amounts I shall certainly trust you with more. Come and celebrate with me!'

Then the third servant stepped forward and returned to his master exactly what he had been given. His master was furious and said to him, 'You useless, lazy man! Even if you had simply put this amount in the bank, with interest it would have made more!'

He took the talent from his servant and gave it to the other who already had ten. 'To everyone who has something, even more will be given,' he said. 'Those who have little, will have even that taken away.'

Then he had the lazy servant thrown out, while he celebrated with the other two.

This is the Gospel of the Lord
**Praise to you, Lord Jesus Christ**

HEAR THE GOOD NEWS

## CHRIST THE KING

*Matthew 25:31-46*

A reading from the Gospel of St Matthew

Jesus said:

At the end of time the Son of God will come, surrounded by angels, and take his place as King on his royal throne. Every race and generation will stand before him, and he will sort the good from the bad, to the right and to the left, just as a shepherd sorts the sheep from the goats. Then the King of glory will say to those standing on his right, 'Come and take possession of the kingdom which is rightly yours. For when I was hungry, you fed me; when I was thirsty, you gave me a drink; when you did not know me, you made me welcome; when I had nothing to wear, you gave me clothes; when I was ill, you took care of me; when I was imprisoned, you came to visit me.'

And they will ask, 'When did we do all these things for you, Lord?'

'I tell you, whenever you did any of these things for others you did them for me.'

Then he will say to those standing on his left, 'Leave this place and go to the everlasting fire prepared for the devil and his followers, because you turned away and did none of these things for me.'

So they will ask, 'Lord, when did we turn away from you and refuse to love or support you?'

And he will answer, 'Whenever you failed to do

this for anyone, you failed to do it for me. Those who are just and good will enjoy everlasting life, but the others will receive everlasting punishment.'

This is the Gospel of the Lord
**Praise to you, Lord Jesus Christ**

# YEAR B

# First Sunday of Advent

*Mark 13:33-37*

A reading from the Gospel of St Mark

Jesus said:

> Stay awake and be alert, because you have no idea when the Son of Man will come. Think of the man who leaves his servants in charge while he travels abroad. He warns them to watch for his return, whenever that might be, so he doesn't find them sleeping when he returns unexpectedly. So to all of you I say, stay awake and keep yourselves ready!

This is the Gospel of the Lord
**Praise to you, Lord Jesus Christ**

# Second Sunday of Advent

*Mark 1:1-8*

A reading from the Gospel of St Mark

This is the beginning of the Gospel written about Jesus Christ, the Son of God. The prophet Isaiah had written long ago:

> See, I will send my messenger before you
> to prepare your way;
> a single voice calling out in the desert,
> 'Get ready for the Lord who is coming.
> Make a straight path for him!'

So it was that John the Baptist began preaching in the desert, calling the people to make amends for their sins and to be baptised. From as far as Jerusalem and all over Judaea, people came to confess their sins and to be baptised in the River Jordan as a sign of their repentance. John wore a simple camel-hair coat, fastened around the middle with a leather belt, and locusts and wild honey were his food.

As he was preaching one day, he said to the crowd, 'There is someone coming who is much greater than I am, and I am unworthy even to kneel at his feet and undo his sandals. I have baptised you with water, but he will baptise you with the Holy Spirit.'

This is the Gospel of the Lord
**Praise to you, Lord Jesus Christ**

# Third Sunday of Advent

*John 1:6-8, 19-28*

A reading from the Gospel of St John

God sent a man whose name was John. He came as a messenger, to tell the people about the light, so that through him they would believe in that light. He himself was not the light, but simply a messenger sent on behalf of the light.

The Jews sent some priests to John the Baptist to ask him, 'Who are you?'

'I am not the promised one,' he answered.

'Are you Elijah or a prophet?' they asked.

'No, I am neither of these,' he replied.

'Well, who are you then, and why are you baptising these people?'

John answered using the words of the prophet Isaiah, 'I am a voice crying out in the desert, "Prepare a way for the Lord!" I baptise you with water, but there is one you do not yet know, who stands among you – one who is coming after me. I am not fit even to undo his sandals.'

All this occurred at a place called Bethany, where John had been baptising people in the River Jordan.

This is the Gospel of the Lord
**Praise to you, Lord Jesus Christ**

# Fourth Sunday of Advent

*Luke 1:26-38*

A reading from the Gospel of St Luke

God sent the angel Gabriel to a town in Galilee called Nazareth, to a young woman there called Mary. She was engaged to marry a carpenter called Joseph, a descendant of King David's family.

The angel greeted Mary with the words, 'Be glad, Mary, for God is with you and has given you great blessings.'

Mary was troubled and wondered what the angel's words meant.

'There is nothing to fear,' Gabriel assured her. 'You will have a son and name him Jesus. He will be called Son of the Most High, whose reign will never end.'

'How can this happen,' asked Mary, 'when I am not married?'

'The Holy Spirit will come to you,' said Gabriel. 'Therefore this child will be holy and be known as the Son of God. Nothing is impossible for God. Your cousin Elizabeth who was childless, is herself expecting a baby.'

Then Mary said, 'I am God's servant, and will do whatever he asks. Let everything happen just as you have said.'

Then the angel left her.

This is the Gospel of the Lord
**Praise to you, Lord Jesus Christ**

# Christmas Day

*Luke 2:1-14*

A reading from the Gospel of St Luke

Caesar Augustus, the Roman Emperor, ordered a census to be taken, and everyone returned to the town of their family origin to be registered. So it was that Joseph and Mary left Nazareth in Galilee and returned to Bethlehem in Judaea, King David's childhood home. This was because Joseph was a descendant of David's royal line.

While they were there, the time came for Mary to have her baby, and she wrapped him in strips of cloth and laid him in a manger, because there was no room at the inn.

On a hillside near the town, some shepherds were watching over their sheep. Suddenly, an angel appeared and the sky was filled with God's glory. The shepherds were terrified, but the angel said, 'Do not be afraid, for I have great news for you. Today a baby has been born in Bethlehem. He is Christ the Lord, and you will find him lying in a manger.'

The sky was filled with the sound of angels singing, 'Glory to God in the highest, and peace to all people on earth!'

This is the Gospel of the Lord
**Praise to you, Lord Jesus Christ**

# THE HOLY FAMILY

*Luke 2:22-40*

A reading from the Gospel of St Luke

Mary and Joseph took Jesus to the Temple to present him to the Lord, and to offer sacrifice as required by the law of Moses. (Every first-born boy must be dedicated to God and a sacrifice of two turtle-doves or a pair of young pigeons must be offered.)

Living in Jerusalem was a man called Simeon who was filled with the Holy Spirit. He had been promised by God that he would not die until he had seen the Christ. The Spirit guided Simeon to the Temple that day, and when he set eyes on Jesus, he took the child in his arms and began to praise God and give him thanks:

> Now Lord, let me die in peace.
> Just as you promised,
> I have seen the Saviour
> you have sent to reveal your love and glory
> not just for your people Israel but for everyone.

Mary and Joseph were full of wonder at everything being said about Jesus. Simeon blessed them both, and, turning to Mary, he said, 'He will cause many in Israel to fall and many to rise, he will be rejected and scorned, and your own heart will be pierced by a terrible sword.'

Anna, the daughter of Phanuel, was an elderly prophetess who lived in the Temple. She spent her life serving God through constant prayer and fasting. As soon as she saw Jesus, Anna began to praise God and tell everyone about the child who would save Jerusalem.

When Mary and Joseph had done everything that the law required, they took Jesus home to Nazareth in Galilee. There he grew into a strong and wise young man, and he was blessed by God.

This is the Gospel of the Lord
**Praise to you, Lord Jesus Christ**

# Second Sunday after Christmas

*John 1:1-18*

A reading from the Gospel of St John

At the beginning of time, the Word already existed. The Word was with God; and the Word was God. From the very beginning, all things were created through him. All life came from the Word, and this life was the light for all people. The light shines out from the darkness, and the darkness could never overcome it.

God sent a man called John, to be a witness for the light, so that others would believe because of him, even though he was not the light. The real light was the Word who was coming into the world to give light to everyone.

He was in the world created through him, and yet the world did not know him. He came to his own people and they did not accept him. To those who did receive him he gave the right to become children of God, the offspring of God himself.

The Word became flesh and he lived as a man among us. We saw his glory given by the Father to his only Son, who is full of grace and truth.

John came to be his witness and he said: 'This is the one whom I spoke of when I said, "He who succeeds me, has passed before me, because he already existed." We received God's law through Moses, but it is through Jesus Christ that we receive many gifts and his grace and truth. God has never been seen, but Jesus, his only beloved son, has made God known to us as never before, because he is very close to his Father's heart.'

This is the Gospel of the Lord
**Praise to you, Lord Jesus Christ**

# THE EPIPHANY OF THE LORD

*Matthew 2:1-12*

A reading from the Gospel of St Matthew

Jesus was born in Bethlehem, a small town in Judaea when King Herod ruled the land. Some wise men from the east travelled to Jerusalem and asked King Herod where they could find the new-born King of the Jews whom they had come to worship.

Herod was greatly troubled because he didn't want anyone else to be king, so he sent for his advisers. 'Tell me where this child, the so-called King, will be born,' he said.

'It has been foretold by the prophets that he will be born in Bethlehem,' they answered.

For the prophets had written:
> And you, Bethlehem in Judaea,
> are not the least important among Judaean cities,
> for from you a leader will come,
> a shepherd for my people Israel!

King Herod sent for the wise men privately, and asked them to tell him exactly when the star had first appeared. Then he said to them, 'I will allow you to search for this child, but you must come back and tell me where to find him. Then I too can go and honour him.'

The wise men set off again on their journey. They followed the bright star until it appeared to stop over a house, where they found Mary with the baby Jesus. They were filled with wonder and joy, and, falling to their knees to worship him, they gave him gifts of gold, frankincense and myrrh.

An angel warned them in a dream not to return

to Herod's palace, so they went back to their own country a different way.

This is the Gospel of the Lord
**Praise to you, Lord Jesus Christ**

# The Baptism of the Lord

*Mark 1:7-11*

A reading from the Gospel of St Mark

As he was preaching, John the Baptist said to the crowd, 'There is someone coming who is much greater than I am, and I am unworthy even to kneel at his feet and undo his sandals. I have baptised you with water, but he will baptise you with the Holy Spirit.'

Not long afterwards Jesus came to John from Nazareth in Galilee, to be baptised in the River Jordan. As Jesus emerged from the water, he saw the heavens open and the Spirit of God came down and rested on him like a dove.

Then a voice from heaven said, 'You are my beloved Son, with whom I am well pleased.'

This is the Gospel of the Lord
**Praise to you, Lord Jesus Christ**

# First Sunday of Lent

*Mark 1:12-15*

A reading from the Gospel of St Mark

The Spirit led Jesus into the desert among the wild animals where he stayed for forty days, and the devil came to tempt him, while angels watched over him.

Soon after John the Baptist's arrest, Jesus travelled throughout Galilee proclaiming the Gospel and saying to the people, 'The kingdom of God is very near! Turn away from sin and believe the Good News.'

This is the Gospel of the Lord
**Praise to you, Lord Jesus Christ**

YEAR B

# Second Sunday of Lent

*Mark 9:2-10*

A reading from the Gospel of St Mark

Jesus led Peter, James and John to the top of a high mountain where they could be alone. While they looked on, Jesus' appearance was transformed as his clothes shone brilliantly white. Then Elijah and Moses appeared before them and began talking to Jesus.

The disciples were so afraid they did not know what to do or say, until Peter spoke up. 'Master, it is wonderful for us to be here. We could make a shelter for each one of you!'

At that moment a passing cloud covered them with its shadow, and a voice came from the cloud and said, 'This is my Son whom I love very much. Listen to what he says.'

Then suddenly they found themselves alone with Jesus, who told them not to tell anyone what they had seen until the Son of Man had risen from the dead. They did what Jesus asked, but discussed amongst themselves what 'rising from the dead' could possibly mean.

This is the Gospel of the Lord
**Praise to you, Lord Jesus Christ**

# Third Sunday of Lent

*John 2:13-25*

A reading from the Gospel of St John

Jesus went to Jerusalem to celebrate the Jewish Passover. He found the Temple in Jerusalem full of people selling cattle, sheep and pigeons, and amongst them sat the money-changers.

He was very angry and overturned the tables of the money-changers, scattering their coins everywhere. Using a whip he angrily chased the animals and the merchants out of the Temple shouting at them, 'Take all of these things away and stop making my Father's house into a market place!'

The Temple priests tried to stop Jesus and asked, 'What right do you have to act like this?'

Jesus answered, 'Destroy this Temple and I will raise it again in three days.'

'This Temple took forty-six years to build! How could you rebuild it in three days!' they exclaimed.

But the temple which Jesus spoke of was his own body, and after his resurrection from the dead, his disciples would understand what Jesus had said that day. Many people saw the signs Jesus worked while he was in Jerusalem, and they believed in him. Since Jesus knew what was in the hearts and minds of the people, he was careful whom he trusted.

This is the Gospel of the Lord
**Praise to you, Lord Jesus Christ**

# Fourth Sunday of Lent

*John 3:14-21*

A reading from the Gospel of St John

Jesus said to Nicodemus:

> Just as Moses raised up the bronze snake in the desert, so the Son of Man must be raised up, so that everyone who believes in him may have eternal life.
>
> God loved the world so much that he sent his only Son to give eternal life to those who believe in him.
>
> He was not sent to judge the world but to be its saviour. Those who choose not to believe in him have determined their own judgement. The light of the world has come, but many turn away from it and prefer the darkness. Anyone who does wrong is afraid of the light, because their badness will be plain for all to see. Good people are not afraid of the light, because it shows that what they do, comes from God.

This is the Gospel of the Lord
**Praise to you, Lord Jesus Christ**

# Fifth Sunday of Lent

*John 12:20-33*

A reading from the Gospel of St John

Some Greeks who had come to Jerusalem to celebrate the approaching Passover feast came to Philip and asked to meet Jesus. Philip told this to Andrew, and the two disciples went to tell Jesus.

Jesus said to them, 'The time has come for the Son of Man to be glorified. Just as a grain of wheat must die to produce a harvest of many grains, so the Son of God must die so that many can live. Whoever hates his earthly life will keep it for eternal life. If someone wants to serve me, then they must be prepared to follow me. If they do this, then my heavenly Father will glorify them.'

Jesus was troubled because he knew the time for him to die was fast approaching. 'Should I ask my Father to stop this from happening, when it was for this very reason that I have come? Father, glory be to your name!'

Then a voice spoke from the clouds and said, 'My name has been glorified, and will be again!' The crowd heard the voice, but thought it was the sound of thunder. So Jesus said, 'This voice has spoken for your sake. Now it is judgement time for this world; the prince of this world will be overthrown, and when I am raised up I will gather everyone to myself.'

In this way, Jesus revealed how he would die.

This is the Gospel of the Lord
**Praise to you, Lord Jesus Christ**

# Palm (Passion) Sunday – Liturgy of the Palms

*Mark 11:1-10*

A reading from the Gospel of St Mark

As Jesus and his disciples drew close to Jerusalem, they stopped near the villages of Bethphage and Bethany, and he sent two of his disciples to one of these villages to collect a colt they found tethered there.

'If anyone questions you,' Jesus said, 'tell them that your Master needs it, and will return it immediately.'

They did as he instructed and repeated everything they had been told to say. They brought the young colt to him, and after throwing a cloak on its back, Jesus climbed on, and continued on his journey to Jerusalem.

Many people had lined the road to greet Jesus, and they spread their cloaks on the road before him, and waved branches in the air, as they shouted with joy, 'Hosanna! Blessed is the one who comes in the name of the Lord.'

This is the Gospel of the Lord
**Praise to you, Lord Jesus Christ**

# Palm (Passion) Sunday – Liturgy of the Passion

*Longer version – Mark 14:1-15:47*

A reading from the Gospel of St Mark

There were only two days left before the festival of Passover, and the chief priests and scribes were still looking for an excuse to have Jesus arrested and executed. They were afraid to do this during the celebrations, in case the people turned against them and rioted, so they plotted to do it in secret.

While Jesus was in Bethany, he stayed with a man called Simon, who had once suffered from a terrible skin disease. As they sat together eating, a woman came to Jesus, carrying a jar of precious ointment called nard. She broke the jar, and poured some of the sweetly perfumed ointment on to his head.

Some of the people were shocked by such extravagant use of expensive ointment and grumbled aloud, 'This ointment could have been sold, and the money given to the poor.'

Jesus said to them, 'Leave her alone! Do not trouble her, because she has done something beautiful for me. You will always have the poor to care for, and you can be good to them whenever you choose, but you will not always have me. She has done what she could, and anointed me in readiness for my burial. Her actions today will be remembered, for all time, wherever the Gospel is proclaimed.'

Meanwhile one of the twelve called Judas Iscariot had gone secretly to the chief priests and offered to find a way to hand Jesus over to them. They were delighted, and agreed to pay him for his help, so Judas went away and waited for his opportunity.

The disciples came to Jesus and asked him where they should go to prepare the Passover meal. Jesus sent two of them into Jerusalem with these instructions: 'When you see a man carrying a water jar, follow him home, and speak to the owner of the house he enters. Ask him to show you the room were your master can share the Passover with his disciples. He will show you a large furnished room with everything you need to prepare for the meal.'

The disciples did what Jesus had told them to do, and everything happened just as he had said.

Later that evening, Jesus and his disciples shared the Passover meal that had been carefully prepared for them. While they were eating, Jesus told his friends, 'I am about to be betrayed by one of you sharing this very meal with me.'

The disciples were upset by these words, and one after another they asked Jesus, 'Lord, you do not mean me, do you?'

Jesus replied, 'It will be one of you who even now dips his bread into the same bowl as I do. It would be better for my betrayer that he had never been born.'

As they were eating, Jesus took some bread which he blessed and broke. Then he shared it with them saying these words, 'Take this, for it is my body.'

Next he blessed a cup of wine, and again he shared it with the disciples, saying to them, 'This is my blood, poured out for many, which seals God's new covenant. I will not drink this wine again, until I drink the new wine in God's kingdom.'

When they had sung a psalm together, Jesus and his disciples made their way to the Mount of Olives on the outskirts of the city. On the way he said to them, 'Just as the Scripture says, you will all be scattered like sheep when the shepherd is struck, but I will go to Galilee and see you there after my resurrection.'

Hearing this, Peter said to Jesus, 'Lord, whatever happens, I will never desert you.'

Jesus answered sadly, 'Before the cock crows at dawn, Peter, you will have disowned me three times.'

'Nonsense, Lord,' Peter replied. 'Even if I have to die with you, I will never desert you.' And all the others said the same.

When they reached the Garden of Gethsemane, Jesus told his disciples to wait for him while he went to pray. Taking Peter, James and John with him, Jesus said to them, 'Keep watch with me and pray, my friends, for tonight my heart is heavy.'

Jesus was filled with great fear and sorrow at the thought of his approaching death. He moved a little further away, before throwing himself on the ground and praying, 'Father, everything is possible for you. Save me from this suffering, but if it is your will, then I will do whatever you ask.'

When he returned to his friends, Jesus was saddened to find them asleep. 'Could you not stay awake and pray with me?' he asked. 'Keep watch and pray you don't give in to sleep.'

Once more he went off alone to pray, and once more he returned to find his companions fast asleep. When this happened for a third time, Jesus said to them, 'Now you have slept enough! The time has come for the Son of Man to be betrayed and handed over.'

At that very moment, Judas arrived with a crowd sent by the religious leaders, armed with swords and clubs. Judas had arranged with them to arrest the man he greeted with a kiss, so he went up to Jesus and said to him, 'Master!' before kissing him.

Immediately the men in the crowd seized hold of Jesus. One of the disciples drew his sword and struck off the ear of the high priest's slave.

Jesus asked his captors, 'Why do you need weapons to arrest me like a common thief? Did you not have every opportunity when I sat openly preaching in the Temple each day?'

Everything had happened this way to fulfil the words of Scripture. All except one young man fled in terror when Jesus was arrested, and even he ran away when the guards tried to arrest him as well.

Jesus was taken by armed escort to the high priest's palace, where the chief priests and scribes were waiting for him. Peter followed behind at a distance, and stood warming himself by the fire in the courtyard.

Meanwhile, the chief priests and members of the Sanhedrin (the powerful Jewish Council) searched for evidence against Jesus. Some witnesses lied about things he had said or done; some reported hearing Jesus say that he would destroy the Temple and rebuild it in three days, and they argued angrily without agreement amongst themselves.

Jesus stood silently and said nothing to defend himself.

Then Caiaphas, the high priest, asked Jesus, 'Tell me, are you indeed the Christ, the Son of God?'

'I am,' Jesus replied, 'and you will see the Son of Man seated on God's right hand.'

At these words Caiaphas leapt to his feet and tore his clothes. 'We have no need of witnesses now,' he cried loudly. 'We have heard this evidence with our own ears! This man has insulted God, and the punishment for such blasphemy is death! What is your verdict?'

Then the whole assembly agreed that he deserved to die, and some of them spat on him and hit him. Jesus was blindfolded and the guards took him away and beat him.

While all this was happening, Peter stood outside in the courtyard. One of the servant girls recognised him and asked, 'Weren't you with Jesus from Galilee?'

Peter denied knowing Jesus and moved away. The servant girl was not convinced, however, and began telling others who he was, but Peter insisted that he did not know Jesus.

By this time a small group of people had gathered, and they said to Peter, 'Surely you come from Galilee, you must be one of his followers.'

Peter became angry and shouted at them, 'God strike me dead, I swear I do not know this man!'

At that very moment, a cock crowed nearby. Peter remembered Jesus' words about disowning him, and he broke down and wept bitterly.

Early that morning Jesus was bound and taken to Pontius Pilate, the Roman governor of Judaea.

Pilate questioned Jesus carefully. 'Is it true that you are the King of the Jews?' he asked.

'It is you who say this,' Jesus replied.

Despite the many accusations made by the chief priests, and the questions Pilate asked, Jesus stood silent and made no attempt to answer any of them. Pilate could find no fault with Jesus, and believed that the Jewish leaders had handed him over out of jealousy.

During the Passover celebrations it was the custom for a prisoner chosen by the people to be released from prison. Urged on by the chief priests, the crowd began to call for the release of Barabbas, a murderer who had fought against the Roman occupation.

'What should I do with the prisoner called Jesus?' Pilate asked them.

The crowd called back, 'Crucify him! Crucify him!'

'Why? What has he done wrong?' asked Pilate.

But they just shouted louder.

To calm the crowd, Pilate agreed to free Barabbas and gave orders for Jesus to be flogged and then crucified.

The Roman soldiers led Jesus away, and they began to taunt and mock him. They dressed him in a purple robe, and pressed a crown of thorns on to his head. Then they knelt before him and said, 'Hail, King of the Jews', and they beat him with a stick and spat on him. When they had had enough of teasing and abusing him, they stripped him of his purple robe and dressed him in his own clothes, before leading him away to be crucified.

The soldiers forced a man called Simon, who came from Cyrene, to help Jesus carry his cross to a place called Golgotha, which means 'the place of the skull'. They offered him wine mixed with myrrh, which he refused to drink.

At nine o'clock in the morning they crucified him, together with two thieves who hung on crosses on either side of him. As the soldiers threw dice to see who would get his clothes, passers-by jeered at Jesus and laughed at the sign above his head which read, 'King of the Jews'.

'If you can destroy the Temple and rebuild it in three days,' they said, 'surely you can get down from the cross!'

The chief priests and scribes also mocked him. 'He saved others,' they said, 'but he can't save himself. Let this Christ come down from the cross, so we can see and believe.'

It was about midday when the sky grew black across the land for three hours. Jesus cried aloud, 'My God, my God, why have you deserted me?'

Hearing this, some of the onlookers thought that he was calling out to the prophet Elijah, and they offered him a sponge soaked with vinegar to wet his lips. But with a loud cry Jesus' final breath left his lifeless body.

At the that moment, the veil which guarded the most holy place in the Temple was torn down the middle. Seeing how Jesus had died, the soldier guarding him said, 'Truthfully, he was the Son of God!'

Many of the women who had followed Jesus from Galilee to care for him watched all this happen from a distance. They included Mary of Magdala, the mother of James and Joseph (also called Mary), and Salome.

As evening fell, Joseph, a member of the council, arrived from Arimathea. It was the day before the Sabbath, and Joseph went to Pilate to ask for the body of Jesus. When a soldier's report confirmed that Jesus was indeed dead, Pilate allowed Joseph to take his body down, and he wrapped it in a clean shroud. He laid Jesus in a tomb chiselled out of the rock, and rolled a large stone across the entrance. Some of the women sat nearby and saw where the body of Jesus was laid to rest.

This is the Gospel of the Lord
**Praise to you, Lord Jesus Christ**

# Palm (Passion) Sunday – Liturgy of the Passion

*Shorter version – Mark 15:1-39*

A reading from the Gospel of St Mark

Early that morning Jesus was bound and taken to Pontius Pilate, the Roman governor of Judaea. Pilate questioned Jesus carefully. 'Is it true that you are the King of the Jews?' he asked. 'It is you who say this,' Jesus replied. Despite the many accusations made by the chief priests, and the questions Pilate asked, Jesus stood silent and made no attempt to answer any of them. Pilate could find no fault with Jesus, and believed that the Jewish leaders had handed him over out of jealousy.

During the Passover celebrations it was the custom for a prisoner chosen by the people to be released from prison. Urged on by the chief priests the crowd began to call for the release of Barabbas, a murderer who had fought against the Roman occupation.

'What should I do with the prisoner called Jesus?' Pilate asked them.

The crowd called back, 'Crucify him! Crucify him!'

'Why? What has he done wrong?' asked Pilate.

But they just shouted louder.

To pacify the crowd, Pilate agreed to free Barabbas and gave orders for Jesus to be flogged and then crucified.

The Roman soldiers led Jesus away, and they

began to taunt and mock him. They dressed him in a purple robe, and pressed a crown of thorns on to his head. Then they knelt before him and said, 'Hail, King of the Jews', and they beat him with a stick and spat on him. When they had had enough of teasing and abusing him, they stripped him of his purple robe and dressed him in his own clothes. Then they led Jesus away to be crucified.

The soldiers forced a man called Simon, who came from Cyrene, to help Jesus carry his cross to a place called Golgotha, which means 'the place of the skull'. They offered him wine mixed with myrrh, which he refused to drink.

At nine o'clock in the morning they crucified him, together with two thieves who hung on crosses on either side of him. As the soldiers threw dice to see who would get his clothes, passers-by jeered at Jesus and laughed at the sign above his head which read, 'King of the Jews.'

'If you can destroy the Temple and rebuild it in three days,' they said, 'surely you can get down from the cross!'

The chief priests and scribes also mocked him. 'He saved others,' they said, 'but he can't save himself. Let this Christ come down from the cross, so we can see and believe.'

It was about midday when the sky grew black across the land for three hours. Jesus cried aloud, 'My God, my God, why have you deserted me?'

Hearing this, some of the onlookers thought that he was calling out to the prophet Elijah, and they offered him a sponge soaked with vinegar to wet his lips. But with a loud cry Jesus' final breath left his lifeless body.

This is the Gospel of the Lord
**Praise to you, Lord Jesus Christ**

YEAR B

# Easter Day

*John 20:1-9*

A reading from the Gospel of St John

Before sunrise on the Sunday morning Mary of Magdala went to the tomb. As she reached the entrance, she saw that the stone had been rolled away and the tomb was empty. She ran to the disciples saying, 'They have taken the Lord from the tomb and we don't know where they have put him!'

Peter and another disciple, John, ran to the tomb and found it just as Mary had described, with the linen burial cloths lying on the ground. The cloth which had been wrapped around Jesus' head lay rolled up separately from the other pieces of cloth. Peter went into the tomb first, followed by John.

Until this moment they had not understood the Scriptures which had said, 'He must rise from the dead.' But now they saw, and they believed.

This is the Gospel of the Lord
**Praise to you, Lord Jesus Christ**

# EASTER DAY

*Alternative reading – Mark 16:1-7*

A reading from the Gospel of St Mark

Early on the Sunday morning, the day after the Sabbath, some of the women made their way to the tomb to anoint Jesus with burial spices. They were Mary, the mother of James, Mary of Magdala and Salome.

On the way there they had been wondering how they would roll back the heavy stone which covered the entrance to the tomb, and when they arrived they were surprised to see that someone had already done this.

Going into the tomb, they were amazed to find a young man, dressed in white, sitting there. Seeing their expressions of surprise, he said to them, 'You have come to find Jesus who was crucified, but he is not where they laid him. He is risen! Go back to Peter and his disciples and tell them he is going ahead of them to Galilee, and, just as he said, you will see him there.'

This is the Gospel of the Lord
**Praise to you, Lord Jesus Christ**

YEAR B

# Second Sunday of Easter

*John 20:19-31*

A reading from the Gospel of St John

On the Sunday after Jesus had died, his disciples gathered together in a locked room, hidden away for fear of being arrested.

Suddenly Jesus appeared in the room with them. 'Peace be with you,' he said, and he showed them the wounds in his hands and his side.

The disciples were overjoyed to see their master again.

'As my Father sent me, so I am sending you,' he said. Then, breathing on them , he said, 'Receive the Holy Spirit, and know that whoever you forgive, I will forgive also!'

The disciple called Thomas was not with the others when Jesus had appeared, and because he had not seen him with his own eyes, he did not believe that Jesus was alive.

A week later Jesus appeared to them again and, greeting them with the words, 'Peace be with you', he showed his wounds to Thomas, and said, 'See the wounds in my hands and side, touch them and doubt no longer, Thomas.'

At once Thomas answered, 'My Lord and my God.'

Jesus said to him, 'You believe because you have seen me with your own eyes. Blessed are those who have not seen and yet believe.'

The disciples of Jesus saw many other marvellous things done by Jesus which are not written down here. What has been included in this book has been written so that you may believe that Jesus is the Christ, the Son of God, and that through this belief in him you will have life.

This is the Gospel of the Lord
**Praise to you, Lord Jesus Christ**

YEAR B

# THIRD SUNDAY OF EASTER

*Luke 24:35-48*

A reading from the Gospel of St Luke

The disciples who had met Jesus on the road to Emmaus were telling the others what had happened, and how they had recognised Jesus in the breaking of bread. Suddenly Jesus appeared among them, and at first they were terrified, because they thought that they had seen a ghost!

Then Jesus said to them, 'Peace be with you.' Seeing that they were still scared, he added, 'Do not be afraid. Why do you doubt what you can see? Look at my wounds and see that I am not a ghost. Touch me, a ghost has no flesh or bones as I have!'

They were overjoyed but still filled with disbelief, so Jesus asked them for something to eat and they watched as he ate some grilled fish.

Then he began to explain the Scriptures to them, and finally they understood what Scripture had said about the Messiah suffering and rising after three days; and how, starting in Jerusalem, the message of repentance and forgiveness should be preached in his name to all the nations.

Then Jesus said to them, 'You are my witnesses because you have seen all these things happen.'

This is the Gospel of the Lord
**Praise to you, Lord Jesus Christ**

# Fourth Sunday of Easter

*John 10:11-18*

A reading from the Gospel of St John

One day Jesus said:

> I am the Good Shepherd, who is ready to die for his sheep. A man who is hired to look after the flock does not really care about it because he knows that the sheep do not belong to him. When the hungry wolf appears, the man runs away, and the sheep are worried or scattered. I know each of my sheep by name, and they know me, just as I know my Father and he knows me. I am ready to give up my life for them, and to lead other sheep who do not belong to this fold. They too will listen to my voice and follow me, so that they become part of one flock which is led by one shepherd. I will give up my life to regain it again, and because of this my Father loves me. No one takes my life from me, because I give it up willingly; that is what my Father has commanded me to do.

This is the Gospel of the Lord
**Praise to you, Lord Jesus Christ**

# Fifth Sunday of Easter

*John 15:1-8*

A reading from the Gospel of St John

Jesus told his disciples:

> I am the true vine and my father is the gardener who tends the vine. Any of my branches which don't bear fruit are cut away, and the branches which carry fruit are pruned by him so that the following year they will produce even more.

> Because you have listened to and understood my message, you will bear much fruit. Through my words I remain in you and you remain in me. A branch that is cut off the vine will wither and die without producing any fruit. I am the vine, and you are the branches; without me you are useless and cannot bear any fruit. But if you stay close to me and carry my words in your heart, then you will bear much fruit and as my disciples, bring glory to my Father in heaven.

This is the Gospel of the Lord
**Praise to you, Lord Jesus Christ**

# Sixth Sunday of Easter

*John 15:9-17*

A reading from the Gospel of St John

One day Jesus said to his disciples:

> I have loved you just as my Father has loved me. If you do what I command, then you will continue in my love just as I continue in my Father's love. I tell you this so that you will be filled with my joy. This is what I command you to do: love each other in the same way as I have loved you. No one can love more than to give up their life for the sake of their friends. You are my friends if you obey my commandments. I no longer call you servants, because servants have no knowledge about their master; because I have shared everything my Father has told me with you, then I call you friends. Now I am sending you out to bear fruit, knowing that my Father will give you whatever you ask for in my name. Remember what I command: love one another.

This is the Gospel of the Lord
**Praise to you, Lord Jesus Christ**

YEAR B

# THE ASCENSION OF THE LORD

*Mark 16:15-20*

A reading from the Gospel of St Mark

Jesus said to his disciples:

> Go out and proclaim the Gospel to the whole world. Whoever is baptised and believes in me, will be saved; whoever does not believe in me will be damned. Whoever believes in me will be recognised by what they are able to do through the power of my name. They shall chase out devils; speak in tongues; poison will not harm them and the sick will be healed.

When he had finished speaking to them, Jesus left his disciples and took his place in heaven at God's right hand.

The disciples did everything Jesus had commanded, and provided signs for all to see, so that they might know that the Lord was indeed with them.

This is the Gospel of the Lord
**Praise to you, Lord Jesus Christ**

## SEVENTH SUNDAY OF EASTER

*John 17:11-19*

A reading from the Gospel of St John

Jesus said:

Holy Father, I pray that you will keep them safe when I have gone, so that they may be one as you and I are one. I have watched over them and kept them safe from harm by the power of your name. Only one was lost to fulfil the words of Scripture. Give them the fullness of my joy, and keep them safe from all evil. Just as you sent me, so I am sending them into the world. For their sake I devote myself to you, so that they might do the same.

This is the Gospel of the Lord
**Praise to you, Lord Jesus Christ**

# PENTECOST SUNDAY

*First reading – Acts 2:1-11*

A reading from the Acts of the Apostles

The disciples had gathered together in Jerusalem to celebrate the Feast of Pentecost and to wait for the Holy Spirit that Jesus had promised to send.

One day, as they were praying together, the room was suddenly filled with the sound of a powerful wind which roared through the house. Then, what looked like small tongues of fire appeared and spread out to touch each one of them. So it was that they were filled with the Holy Spirit.

At once, in their excitement, they rushed outside to tell everyone what had happened to them. As they began to speak, they were amazed to find that everyone listening to their words could understand them! People from different regions and countries were astounded to hear these men preaching to them in their own native languages.

This is the Word of the Lord
**Thanks be to God**

# PENTECOST SUNDAY

*Gospel – John 15:26-27; 16:12-15*

A reading from the Gospel of St John.

Jesus said:

> I will send the Spirit of truth from the Father to be my witness, just as you who have been with me from the beginning will also bear witness to me. There is still much to tell you, but for now you have heard enough. The Spirit will guide you to the truth, and help you to understand all that is yet to come. Through him I shall be glorified, just as the Father is glorified, since all that is mine comes from him.

This is the Gospel of the Lord
**Praise to you, Lord Jesus Christ**

# Trinity Sunday

*Matthew 28:16-20*

A reading from the Gospel of St Matthew

The eleven apostles set off for Galilee to meet Jesus where he had arranged. When Jesus appeared before them on the mountain, several of the apostles fell to their knees and worshipped him; but some doubted.

Then he said to them:

> I have been given authority over everything in heaven and on earth, and by this authority I am sending you out to all peoples to teach them everything I have taught you. Make them my disciples and baptise them in the name of the Father, the Son and the Holy Spirit. Remember that I will never leave you; I am with you until the end of time.

This is the Gospel of the Lord
**Praise to you, Lord Jesus Christ**

# SECOND SUNDAY OF THE YEAR

*John 1:35-42*

A reading from the Gospel of St John

John the Baptist was standing with two of his followers when he saw Jesus walking by. 'There is the Lamb of God,' he said, looking at Jesus.

On hearing this, the two men left John and followed Jesus.

Seeing that they were following him, Jesus turned and asked, 'What do you want?'

'Rabbi, we would like to know where you live,' they answered.

'Come with me and see,' Jesus said.

So they followed him to his house and stayed with him for the rest of the day. One of these disciples, Andrew, was the brother of Simon Peter. Immediately Andrew hurried to find his brother to tell him that he had met the Messiah promised by God.

Simon went with Andrew, and when Jesus saw him he said, 'Simon, son of John, you will be known as *Cephas*, a word which means *rock*.'

This is the Gospel of the Lord
**Praise to you, Lord Jesus Christ**

# Third Sunday of the Year

*Mark 1:14-20*

A reading from the Gospel of St Mark

After John the Baptist had been arrested by Herod, Jesus began to preach to the crowds and proclaim the Good News. One day, while walking beside the sea of Galilee, he saw Simon and his brother Andrew casting their nets to catch fish. Jesus called out to them 'Come, follow me and I will make you fishers of people.'

The brothers left their nets and followed him.

Further along the shore Jesus saw James and his brother John who were mending nets with their father Zebedee. Jesus called them too, and at once they left their father and followed him.

This is the Gospel of the Lord
**Praise to you, Lord Jesus Christ**

# Fourth Sunday of the Year

*Mark 1:21-28*

A reading from the Gospel of St Mark

Jesus was staying in a town called Capernaum, and on the Sabbath day he went to the synagogue to pray. There he began to teach the people, and they were amazed because he spoke to them of God in a way that no one else had ever done before.

Suddenly Jesus was interrupted by a man who was disturbed by an evil spirit. He shouted loudly, 'Jesus of Nazareth, do you want to destroy us? I know you are a holy messenger from God!' and everyone was afraid.

Jesus said in a firm voice, 'Be quiet, spirit, and leave this man in peace.'

The man began to shake, and then with a loud cry, the spirit left him.

Everyone was amazed by what had taken place. 'What is happening?' they asked. 'This man Jesus can explain Scriptures like no one else, and even the spirits will obey him.'

Soon Jesus was famous throughout Galilee as news of his authority and power spread from town to town.

This is the Gospel of the Lord
**Praise to you, Lord Jesus Christ**

# Fifth Sunday of the Year

*Mark 1:29-39*

A reading from the Gospel of St Mark

Jesus left the synagogue and went to the house where Simon Peter and his brother Andrew lived.

When they arrived at the house Jesus was told that Simon Peter's mother-in-law had been taken ill and was suffering from a fever. Jesus went to her, took her by the hand and, as he helped her up, the fever disappeared and she felt well again.

That evening crowds of sick people gathered around Simon Peter's house, and Jesus cured many of them.

Very early the next morning Jesus went off to a lonely place to pray by himself. When Simon Peter woke up and found that Jesus had gone, he set off with his friends to search for him.

'Lots of people are looking for you,' Simon Peter told Jesus when he found him.

Jesus said to them, 'We must go to other towns and villages, because I came to preach the Good News to everyone.'

So Jesus and his companions travelled throughout Galilee, preaching in the synagogues and driving out evil spirits.

This is the Gospel of the Lord
**Praise to you, Lord Jesus Christ**

# Sixth Sunday of the Year

*Mark 1:40-45*

A reading from the Gospel of St Mark

One day a man suffering from an infectious skin disease came to Jesus, and, falling on his knees, he pleaded with Jesus, 'If you really wanted to, you could help me by curing my disease.'

Jesus was filled with compassion and reaching out to touch him he said, 'Of course I want to help you!'

At that moment the disease disappeared and the man was cured. Jesus sent him away, commanding him not to tell anyone else about what had happened but instead to show himself to the priest and make an offering of thanks. But the man was so overjoyed he told everyone he met, and soon crowds of people followed Jesus wherever he travelled, and he could not go into a town without being mobbed.

This is the Gospel of the Lord
**Praise to you, Lord Jesus Christ**

# Seventh Sunday of the Year

*Mark 2:1-12*

A reading from the Gospel of St Mark

When Jesus returned to Capernaum, news soon spread that he was there, and crowds of people gathered outside the house where he was staying.

As Jesus was preaching, four men carrying a stretcher arrived. The man on the stretcher was paralysed and could not walk, and his friends hoped that Jesus would cure him. Because the crowds were so large they could not carry the stretcher close to Jesus. So they climbed on to the roof and made a hole above where Jesus was standing. Then they lowered the stretcher down gently on long ropes.

Seeing their faith, Jesus turned to the man on the stretcher and said to him, 'My son, your sins are forgiven.'

Some of the scribes who were there were shocked and angry when they heard what Jesus had said. 'Who does he think he is!' they exclaimed. 'Only God has the power to forgive sins.'

Knowing what they were thinking, Jesus asked, 'Is it easier to forgive this man's sins, or to make him walk? If you need proof that I have the power to forgive sins, then I shall say to this man, "Stand up! Pick up your stretcher and walk!"'

The man then got to his feet and began to walk.

The people were amazed by this, and began praising God! 'Never have we seen anything like it!' they said.

This is the Gospel of the Lord
**Praise to you, Lord Jesus Christ**

# Eighth Sunday of the Year

*Mark 2:18-22*

A reading from the Gospel of St Mark

One day when the disciples of John the Baptist and the Pharisees were fasting, some of them noticed that Jesus and his disciples were not, and they asked Jesus, 'Why are you eating while everyone else is fasting?'

Jesus answered:

> The friends of the bridegroom will not fast while he is still with them. There will be plenty of time to fast when he has gone. You would not sew a patch of new material on to an old cloak, because when it was washed the patch would shrink and tear the cloak. In the same way no one would pour new wine into old wineskins, because they would burst and the wine and the skins would be lost for ever, so new wine must only be poured into new wineskins.

This is the Gospel of the Lord
**Praise to you, Lord Jesus Christ**

# Ninth Sunday of the Year

*Mark 2:23-3:6*

A reading from the Gospel of St Mark

It was the Jewish Sabbath. Jesus and his disciples took a walk through some cornfields and they picked ears of corn as they went. Seeing what the disciples had done, the Pharisees came to Jesus and said angrily, 'What they have done is forbidden on the Sabbath!'

Jesus reminded the Pharisees that when David and his followers needed something to eat they had gone into God's house and eaten the bread given as an offering. 'The law allowed only the priests to eat such bread,' he said, 'but David ate it and shared it with his followers too.'

Then Jesus said to the Pharisees, 'People were not made for the Sabbath, instead the Sabbath was made for people; and the Son of Man is master of even the Sabbath.'

On another occasion, again when it was the Sabbath day, Jesus and his disciples went to the synagogue. A man with a paralysed hand was there, and the Pharisees watched carefully to see whether Jesus would ignore the rules of the Sabbath and cure him. Jesus knew what they were thinking, so he called the man forward and asked the Pharisees, 'What does the law allow us to do on the Sabbath day? To do a good deed or a bad one; to save someone's life or to end it?'

They did not answer him, and he was annoyed because they were so set in their ways.

Jesus turned to the paralysed man and said, 'Hold

out your hand.' The man did so, and at once he was cured.

The Pharisees went away and began planning how to get rid of Jesus.

This is the Gospel of the Lord
**Praise to you, Lord Jesus Christ**

# TENTH SUNDAY OF THE YEAR

*Mark 3:20-35*

A reading from the Gospel of St Mark

Jesus returned home, and before long a large crowd had gathered, eager to hear him teaching and to see if all they had heard about him was true. There were so many there that it was impossible for Jesus even to have a meal. When his relatives heard about this, they set off to take charge of the situation which they believed had got out of hand!

Some scribes from Jerusalem were among the crowd that had gathered, and they mumbled to themselves, 'He is able to chase devils out of people, through the power of the devil himself!'

Then Jesus spoke to them in parables saying:

> How can the devil cast out the devil? If you divide a kingdom or a household into many parts which argue with each other, then they will be weak and cannot last. If the devil is divided against himself, then he will not last either. No one can rob a strong man's house unless he has first been tied up.

Because they had accused him of having an unclean spirit in him, Jesus said to them, 'All things can be forgiven, but treating the Holy Spirit with disrespect is unforgivable.'

When the family of Jesus arrived, they sent a message to him, saying, 'Your family are outside, waiting to see you.'

Jesus said to the people sitting around him, 'Who

is my family? All of you are my brothers and sisters! Anyone who does what God wants them to do will truly belong to my family!'

This is the Gospel of the Lord
**Praise to you, Lord Jesus Christ**

# Eleventh Sunday of the Year

*Mark 4:26-34*

A reading from the Gospel of St Mark

Jesus said to his disciples:

> The kingdom of heaven is like a man who scatters seed in his field. Hour by hour, through daylight and darkness, the seeds send out shoots and roots, and begin to grow. The man does not know how this all happens, but before long his field is full of crops, and when the harvest is ripe the man begins to reap what he has sown.

> Or compare the kingdom of heaven to a tiny mustard seed, which becomes one of the largest shrubs, and the birds of the air can find shelter in its many branches.

Jesus told the people many parables, and later when he was alone with his disciples he helped them to understand what they meant.

This is the Gospel of the Lord
**Praise to you, Lord Jesus Christ**

# Twelfth Sunday of the Year

*Mark 4:35-41*

A reading from the Gospel of St Mark

Jesus and his disciples set off to sail to the other side of the Sea of Galilee. Jesus had been preaching all day, and he was soon lulled to sleep by the rocking of the boat. Suddenly a storm blew up, and great waves began to pound the boat. The disciples were terrified and ran to wake Jesus before they all drowned.

Jesus got up and, scolding the sea and wind, he said, 'Be at peace!'

At once the wind dropped and the sea grew calm again. Then Jesus asked his disciples, 'Why were you so afraid? Did you not believe in me?'

They were filled with wonder because they had seen that even the sea and wind would obey his commands.

This is the Gospel of the Lord
**Praise to you, Lord Jesus Christ**

# THIRTEENTH SUNDAY OF THE YEAR

*Mark 5:21-43*

A reading from the Gospel of St Mark

A large crowd had gathered around Jesus by the lakeside, when a man called Jairus came to him, fell on his knees and pleaded, 'Master, my little girl is dying! Please come and use your healing touch so that she will be well again.'

Jesus set off with Jairus, and a large crowd of people surrounded them as they made their way to Jairus' house. Among them was a woman who had been ill for twelve long years, and none of the doctors she had visited had been able to cure her.

'If I can get close enough just to touch his cloak,' she thought, 'then I believe that Jesus will cure me.'

She pushed her way through the bustling crowd, and, stretching out her hand, she managed to touch Jesus as he passed. At once she knew that she was cured!

Then Jesus asked Peter, 'Who touched me?'

And Peter answered, 'Master, in such a crowd many people have touched you.'

'I felt my power leaving me,' Jesus said.

Then the woman stepped forward, trembling with fear, and said, 'I touched you because I believed that you would cure me and you have!'

Jesus said to the woman, 'Because you believed in me, your faith has made you well. Go in peace!'

While Jesus was speaking to the woman, a servant

came to tell them that the little girl they were on their way to see had died. Jesus turned to Jairus and said, 'Do not be afraid, trust me and have faith.'

At the house everyone was crying and feeling very sad, but Jesus told them, 'Don't cry, the little girl is not dead, only sleeping.'

They laughed at Jesus! But he sent them all outside and then Jesus took Jairus and his wife, and the disciples James, John and Peter, up to the room where the little girl lay.

Taking her hand gently, Jesus said quietly, 'Little girl, get up!'

The little girl, who was twelve years old, got up and walked around the room. They were all so amazed that they didn't know what to say or do next, until Jesus said, 'Give her something to eat, she must be hungry!'

This is the Gospel of the Lord
**Praise to you, Lord Jesus Christ**

# Fourteenth Sunday of the Year

*Mark 6:1-6*

A reading from the Gospel of St Mark

Jesus returned to his home town of Nazareth with his disciples, and on the Sabbath day he went to the synagogue to preach.

The people there were amazed by his wisdom and all that he said, and many of them had heard of the miracles that he had worked. But some of the crowd asked, 'Surely this is Joseph the carpenter's son? Isn't his family still living here in Nazareth? How can he know all these things and talk in this way?'

They would not listen to Jesus or believe in him. Jesus was saddened and disappointed by their lack of faith, and he left Nazareth to go and preach in the surrounding villages.

This is the Gospel of the Lord
**Praise to you, Lord Jesus Christ**

# FIFTEENTH SUNDAY OF THE YEAR

*Mark 6:7-13*

A reading from the Gospel of St Mark

Then Jesus called his twelve apostles together and sent them out in pairs to preach to the people and to cure the sick. He told them to take no money, no spare clothes and no food. 'If someone makes you welcome, then stay with them until your work is finished,' he said. 'But if people are unfriendly and do not want to listen to your message, then walk away and leave them to themselves.'

The apostles set off and did everything as Jesus had said. Many people turned back to God after hearing their words, and others were cured in Jesus' name.

This is the Gospel of the Lord
**Praise to you, Lord Jesus Christ**

# Sixteenth Sunday of the Year

*Mark 6:30-34*

A reading from the Gospel of St Mark

After preaching to the people and curing many who were sick, the apostles returned to Jesus, and told him everything that they had said and done. As usual, crowds of people had followed them, and they were so busy they had no time to eat. So Jesus said to them, 'We will go somewhere quiet and spend some time alone, and they crossed the lake in a boat to a quiet place.'

However, when Jesus and his friends arrived, a crowd of people had already gathered to meet them. When he saw them Jesus was filled with pity, because they were like sheep without a shepherd to care for them. He sat down on the hillside and began to teach them.

This is the Gospel of the Lord
**Praise to you, Lord Jesus Christ**

# Seventeenth Sunday of the Year

*John 6:1-15*

A reading from the Gospel of St John

Jesus crossed the Sea of Galilee, and, seeing that a large crowd had followed him along the shore, he turned to Philip and asked, 'Where can we buy some bread to feed these people?'

Philip answered, 'Master, it would cost a fortune to give each person even a small piece of bread!'

Then Andrew brought to Jesus a young boy who had five loaves and two fish.

'But what use are these,' asked Andrew, 'among all these people?'

'Tell the people to sit down on the grass,' Jesus said, and, taking the bread and fish, he gave thanks to God, then gave the food out to as many as five thousand people, and there was plenty for everyone. When they had finished, they filled twelve baskets with the scraps that were left over from the five loaves and two fish.

Seeing the marvellous miracle worked by Jesus that day, the people were determined to make him their king, so Jesus slipped away into the hills by himself before they could take him by force.

This is the Gospel of the Lord
**Praise to you, Lord Jesus Christ**

# EIGHTEENTH SUNDAY OF THE YEAR

*John 6:24-35*

A reading from the Gospel of St John

When the people realised that the disciples of Jesus had left for Capernaum, they too crossed the sea by boat to look for Jesus there. When they found him, Jesus said to them, 'You came looking for me because I gave you all the bread you could eat. You have not come because you have seen the signs I have given. Do not search for food that goes bad, but for food that will last for ever, which the Son of Man can give you!'

So they asked him, 'What should we do to please God?'

Jesus replied, 'You must believe in the one he sent.'

Then they said to Jesus, 'What sign will you give us so that we can believe in you? Scripture tells us that our fathers were given manna to eat in the desert.'

He answered them, 'It was not Moses who gave you bread from heaven, but my Father, who gives the true bread. The bread of God comes down from heaven and gives life to the world.'

Hearing his words, the people said to Jesus, 'Sir, please give us that bread.'

Jesus looked at them and said, 'I am the bread of life; anyone who comes to me will never go hungry; whoever believes in me will never be thirsty.'

This is the Gospel of the Lord
**Praise to you, Lord Jesus Christ**

## NINETEENTH SUNDAY OF THE YEAR

*John 6:41-51*

A reading from the Gospel of St John

Some of the Jews began grumbling because Jesus had described himself as bread that came from heaven. 'How can he possibly claim to come from heaven,' they said, 'when we know that his parents are Mary and Joseph!'

When Jesus heard their complaints he said to them:

> No one comes to me except through the Father who sent me. Anyone who listens to the Father and learns from his teaching, will come to me. Nobody, except the one sent by him, has seen the Father. Truthfully I tell you, whoever believes has everlasting life. I am the bread of life. Your ancestors who ate manna in the desert are all dead, but anyone who eats the bread from heaven will not die, and I am that living bread. My body is the bread that I shall give to bring life to the world.

This is the Gospel of the Lord
**Praise to you, Lord Jesus Christ**

# Twentieth Sunday of the Year

*John 6:51-58*

A reading from the Gospel of St John

Jesus said to the people, 'I am the bread of life which has come down from heaven. This bread is my body which will be given to save the world, and whoever eats it will live for ever.'

'What nonsense is this?' asked the Jews angrily. 'Are we supposed to eat this man's flesh?'

Then Jesus said:

> Whoever eats my body and drinks my blood will rise up on the last day to share eternal life with God. They will live in me, and I will fill them with my life. Just as my life comes from the Father, so their life will come from me. This bread comes from heaven, and it is not like the bread your fathers ate. They are all dead. But whoever eats the bread of life will live for ever.

This is the Gospel of the Lord
**Praise to you, Lord Jesus Christ**

# Twenty-first Sunday of the Year

*John 6:60-69*

A reading from the Gospel of St John

After hearing what Jesus had said in the synagogue, many of his followers refused to believe what they had heard. When Jesus heard them arguing, he said to them, 'It is not the body but the spirit which gives life! My words are spirit and they give you life.' Then he said, 'Many will not believe that I am the way to eternal life. I know that my heavenly Father has revealed this to only a few.'

After this some of his followers left him and kept his company no more. Jesus turned to the twelve he had chosen and asked, 'Will you leave me too?'

Then Simon Peter stepped forward and said, 'Master, who would we turn to? We believe in your message of eternal life, because we know that you are the Son of God.'

This is the Gospel of the Lord
**Praise to you, Lord Jesus Christ**

# Twenty-second Sunday of the Year

*Mark 7:1-8, 14-15, 21-23*

A reading from the Gospel of St Mark

One day the Pharisees noticed that some of the disciples of Jesus had not washed properly before eating. It was the Jewish custom to wash up to the elbows before eating, and there were many other rules about washing and cleaning which they strictly obeyed. So they asked Jesus, 'Why do you ignore our customs and eat your food with unclean hands?'

Jesus answered:

> Isaiah was right when he foretold of your hypocrisy! You have made the laws of men more important than the laws of God. Listen to me! It is not what goes into a person that makes them unclean, but what comes out of that person. Ordinary dirt cannot make our hearts and lives unclean! Only wicked words, thoughts and actions can do this, because they come from the heart.

This is the Gospel of the Lord
**Praise to you, Lord Jesus Christ**

# Twenty-third Sunday of the Year

*Mark 7:31-37*

A reading from the Gospel of St Mark

Some time later Jesus was returning to the Sea of Galilee when some people brought to him a man who was deaf and could not speak properly, and they asked Jesus to help him.

Jesus led the man away to a quiet place where he touched his ears and tongue with his fingers. Then he looked up to heaven and said, 'Be opened!' At once the man could hear and speak clearly!

Although Jesus told the people to tell no one what had happened, they could not contain their joy and delight. They told everyone they met about the miracle Jesus had performed, saying, 'Everything he does is marvellous, he even makes the deaf hear and the mute speak.'

This is the Gospel of the Lord
**Praise to you, Lord Jesus Christ**

# Twenty-fourth Sunday of the Year

*Mark 8:27-35*

A reading from the Gospel of St Mark

As they made their way together to the villages around Caesarea Philippi, Jesus asked his disciples, 'Who do people say that I am?'

'Some say that you are John the Baptist, or Elijah or a prophet sent by God,' they answered.

Then Jesus asked them, 'Who do you think I am?'

It was Simon Peter who spoke up and said, 'You are the Christ.'

After this Jesus began to tell them how he would suffer and die, but would rise again after three days.

Later, when they were alone, Simon Peter argued with Jesus. 'Lord,' he said, 'these things must never be allowed to happen!'

Jesus scolded Peter, 'The way you think is not God's way! Yours are the thoughts of a man.'

Then Jesus gathered his disciples together and said to them, 'Anyone who wants to follow me must surrender himself and carry his own cross. Whoever gives up his life for me or for the gospel will save it instead.'

This is the Gospel of the Lord
**Praise to you, Lord Jesus Christ**

## TWENTY-FIFTH SUNDAY OF THE YEAR

*Mark 9:30-37*

A reading from the Gospel of St Mark

Jesus made his way through Galilee, taking care to avoid people so that he could spend his time teaching his disciples. He explained to them how he would be betrayed and put to death, before rising from the dead after three days. Even though they did not understand what this meant, they were afraid to ask him to explain.

When they arrived in Capernaum, Jesus asked his disciples what they had been discussing on the way. No one answered his question because they had been arguing about which one of them was the most important.

Jesus told the disciples to sit down and then he said, 'Anyone who wants to be the greatest must become the servant of all, and make himself the least important.'

Then, taking a small child in his arms, Jesus said to them, 'Anyone who welcomes a little child like this in my name welcomes me and in turn the one who sent me.'

This is the Gospel of the Lord
**Praise to you, Lord Jesus Christ**

# Twenty-sixth Sunday of the Year

*Mark 9:38-43, 45, 47-48*

A reading from the Gospel of St Mark

One day John came to Jesus and said, 'Lord, we saw a man curing the sick in your name, and because we did not know him we told him to stop!'

But Jesus said to John:

> Do not stop anyone from performing an act of goodness in my name. Those who do such things are unlikely to speak badly of me. They are not against us, but on our side. Anyone who gives you a drink simply because you are one of my disciples will be rewarded for their kindness. In the same way, anyone who destroys the faith of one of my followers will be punished in hell for their wickedness. It is better to lose something truly important, which you can manage without, than to lose the kingdom of God which is more precious than anything else.

This is the Gospel of the Lord
**Praise to you, Lord Jesus Christ**

# Twenty-seventh Sunday of the Year

*Mark 10:2-16*

A reading from the Gospel of St Mark

Some of the Pharisees came to Jesus and asked him, 'Does the law allow a man to divorce his wife?'

Realising that they were trying to trap him, Jesus asked, 'What did Moses command you to do?'

'Moses allowed a man to dismiss his wife and send her away,' they replied.

Then Jesus said to them, 'Moses gave you this commandment because your hearts were hardened and he could not teach you otherwise. From the very beginning God created male and female; so when a man leaves his family and is joined to his wife, they become one body. No one can separate what God has joined together.'

Later, when the disciples were alone with Jesus, they asked him to explain his answer to the Pharisees.

'If a man divorces his wife and remarries another woman, then he has committed adultery against his wife,' Jesus told them. 'In the same way, if a woman divorces her husband and marries another man, then she too is guilty of adultery.'

People would often bring their children to Jesus to be blessed by him, and on one particular day the disciples sent the children away. But Jesus scolded his disciples and said, 'Let them come to me and do not stand in their way, for God's kingdom belongs to such as these. Anyone wishing to enter the kingdom of God, must first become like one of these little children.'

Then he took the children in his arms and blessed each one of them.

This is the Gospel of the Lord
**Praise to you, Lord Jesus Christ**

# TWENTY-EIGHTH SUNDAY OF THE YEAR

*Mark 10:17-30*

A reading from the Gospel of St Mark

A man came to Jesus and asked, 'Good Master, what must I do if I want to have eternal life?'

Jesus asked him, 'Why do you call me good, when you know that only God is good?' Then he said to the man, 'You already know the commandments given by God. Do not commit murder; do not commit adultery; do not steal or falsely accuse anyone; do not cheat; and always respect your parents.'

'I have always tried to live according to these rules,' the man replied.

Jesus looked at the man kindly, and said, 'Then this is what you must do: sell everything you own, and give all your money away, for by doing this you will have riches in heaven. Then come and follow me.'

The man was sad because he was very wealthy.

When he had gone, Jesus said to his disciples, 'Those who are rich will indeed find it hard to enter God's kingdom.' Seeing the disciples' astonishment, he continued, 'It is not easy for anyone to enter the kingdom of God! But a camel would find it easier to pass through a needle's eye than a rich man would to enter the kingdom of heaven.'

'If this is so,' asked the disciples, 'what hope is there for anyone?'

'Nothing is impossible for God,' Jesus replied.

Hearing what Jesus had said, Peter said to him, 'Master, we have given up everything to follow you.'

Jesus turned to Peter and replied, 'Anyone who leaves their home and family and all that they own because of me and the Gospel I preach will be repaid more than a hundredfold, both in this life and the life to come.

This is the Gospel of the Lord
**Praise to you, Lord Jesus Christ**

# Twenty-ninth Sunday of the Year

*Mark 10:35-45*

A reading from the Gospel of St Mark

The two disciples James and John came to Jesus and asked him, 'Master, can one of us sit on your right and one on your left in the kingdom of heaven?'

Jesus said to them, 'My friends, you do not understand what you are asking. Can you share what I must suffer, and be baptised in the way I shall be baptised?'

'Yes, Lord, we can,' they replied.

'Very well,' said Jesus, 'it shall be so, but only my heavenly Father will decide who sits at my right hand or my left.'

When the other disciples heard what James and John had asked, they were angry and began to argue with them.

> Jesus said to them:
> You must not quarrel with each other about which of you is the greatest! I have come as a servant and not as a king! Anyone who wants to be great, must be ready to serve everyone else; anyone who wants to be first must be ready to put others before them. After all, the Son of Man came to serve others, and to give up his life to set many people free.

This is the Gospel of the Lord
**Praise to you, Lord Jesus Christ**

# THIRTIETH SUNDAY OF THE YEAR

*Mark 10:46-52*

A reading from the Gospel of St Mark

Jesus and his disciples were leaving Jericho with a crowd of followers, when a blind beggar called Bartimaeus was sitting at the roadside. When he heard that Jesus of Nazareth was passing, Bartimaeus began to shout loudly, 'Jesus, son of David, have pity and help me!'

The crowd told him to calm down and be quiet, but Bartimaeus kept on shouting until Jesus heard his cries.

'Bring that man to me,' said Jesus, and they led Bartimaeus to him. 'What do you want me to do for you?' Jesus asked.

Bartimaeus replied, 'Master, give me sight so that I can see!'

Then Jesus told him, 'Go. Because you believe in me your sight has returned.'

Suddenly Bartimaeus could see clearly, and he set off at once to follow Jesus.

This is the Gospel of the Lord
**Praise to you, Lord Jesus Christ**

# Thirty-first Sunday of the Year

*Mark 12:28-34*

A reading from the Gospel of St Mark

One of the scribes came to Jesus and asked, 'Which of God's commandments is the most important?'

Jesus answered, 'To love God with all your heart, and all your soul, and all your mind and all your strength, and to love others as much as you love yourself. These commandments come before all others!'

Then the scribe said to Jesus, 'What you have said is true, because nothing is more important than loving God and loving our neighbours.'

Seeing that the scribe was wise and good, Jesus said to him, 'My friend, you are indeed close to God and his kingdom.'

Hearing this, no one dared to ask Jesus any more questions.

This is the Gospel of the Lord
**Praise to you, Lord Jesus Christ**

# THIRTY-SECOND SUNDAY OF THE YEAR

*Mark 12:38-44*

A reading from the Gospel of St Mark

Jesus said to the people, 'Be wary of the scribes who draw attention to themselves as they walk around in long robes, expecting people to admire and honour them; they are quick to take the best places at a feast; they like to sit at the front in the synagogues. Such men would not hesitate to take advantage of the meek and the poor. They should know better, and will receive the justice they deserve.'

Then Jesus sat down opposite the treasury, and watched the people making their donations. Many of the wealthy Jews gave large amounts of money, but an old woman gave just two small coins, worth as little as one pence. Seeing this, Jesus turned to his disciples and said, 'This old woman has given more than any of the others! They gave only what they could spare, but she has given everything that she had!'

This is the Gospel of the Lord
**Praise to you, Lord Jesus Christ**

# Thirty-third Sunday of the Year

*Mark 13:24-32*

A reading from the Gospel of St Mark

Jesus said to his disciples:

> One day I will return, and you will know that the time has come because of these signs: the sun will grow dark, the moon will lose its brightness, stars will fall to earth and space itself will be shaken. Then the Son of Man will appear in all his glory, and send his angels to gather his people together from every corner of the world. Learn from the fig tree: when its buds appear it is a sign that summer is drawing closer. In the same way, by these signs you will know when the kingdom of God is near. Everything else will pass away, but my words are everlasting. No one except my heavenly Father knows the day or time when all this will happen.

This is the Gospel of the Lord
**Praise to you, Lord Jesus Christ**

# CHRIST THE KING

*John 18:33-37*

A reading from the Gospel of St John

They brought Jesus before Pontius Pilate who asked him, 'Are you the king of the Jews?'

'Is this your own question, or have others suggested it?' replied Jesus.

'Am I a Jew?' Pilate asked impatiently. 'Tell me what you have done wrong to make your own people hand you over to me.'

Then Jesus answered Pilate, 'My kingdom does not belong to this world; if it did, then my people would have fought to save me. My kingdom has no place here!'

'So you do claim to be a king?' asked Pilate again.

'You yourself say it,' Jesus answered. 'This is why I was born into the world: to uphold the truth, and all those who listen to my voice do the same.'

This is the Gospel of the Lord
**Praise to you, Lord Jesus Christ**

# YEAR C

# First Sunday of Advent

*Luke 21:25-28, 34-36*

A reading from the Gospel of St Luke

Jesus said:

> Before the Son of God returns, there will be signs in the sun, moon and stars, and people will be afraid and bewildered by all that they see. There is nothing to fear; instead, give thanks to see the power and glory of God. Hold your heads high because your salvation is near. Stay awake and always keep yourselves ready to meet the Son of God, so that you are not taken by surprise when he comes unexpectedly.

This is the Gospel of the Lord
**Praise to you, Lord Jesus Christ**

## Second Sunday of Advent

*Luke 3:1-6*

A reading from the Gospel of St Luke

When Pontius Pilate was governor of Judaea, a man appeared in the wilderness and began to preach the Word of God; his name was John. He called the people to turn away from sin and to ask for God's forgiveness, and he baptised them as a sign of turning back to God. All this happened just as the prophet Isaiah had foretold:

> A voice cries out in the wilderness,
> prepare a path for the Lord.
> Make it straight and smooth
> and all people will see God's salvation.

This is the Gospel of the Lord
**Praise to you, Lord Jesus Christ**

# Third Sunday of Advent

*Luke 3:10-18*

A reading from the Gospel of St Luke

The people listened to John the Baptist's words and asked him, 'What must we do?'

John told them, 'Be generous and kind, and always ready to share whatever you have with others.' To the tax collectors he said, 'Take no more than you are owed,' and to the soldiers he said, 'Force no one to give you what is not yours. Be content with what you already have.'

The people grew excited and many began to think that John might be the Messiah, promised by God.

But John told them, 'I baptise you with water, but someone is coming who will baptise you with the Holy Spirit. He is filled with the power of God, and I am not good enough to undo his sandals. Just as the wheat and the chaff are separated at harvest time, he will separate the good from the bad.'

This is the Gospel of the Lord
**Praise to you, Lord Jesus Christ**

# Fourth Sunday of Advent

*Luke 1:39-44*

A reading from the Gospel of St Luke

After the angel Gabriel had appeared to Mary, she set off at once to visit her cousin Elizabeth. When Elizabeth saw Mary coming, she ran to welcome her, and the baby inside her leapt for joy at the sound of Mary's greeting.

Elizabeth was filled with the Holy Spirit and said to Mary, 'Of all women you are the most blessed, and blessed is the child you will have, because you believe in the power of God and he has chosen you to be the mother of our Saviour.'

This is the Gospel of the Lord
**Praise to you, Lord Jesus Christ**

# Christmas Day

*Luke 2:15-20*

A reading from the Gospel of St Luke

After the angels had left them, the shepherds hurried to Bethlehem and soon found the stable. There in the manger lay a tiny baby. They told Mary and Joseph what they had seen and heard that night, and they shared their amazement. Mary listened carefully and cherished all these things in her heart. The shepherds went back to their sheep on the hillside, singing God's praises because everything had been as the angel had said.

This is the Gospel of the Lord
**Praise to you, Lord Jesus Christ**

# THE HOLY FAMILY

*Luke 2:41-52*

A reading from the Gospel of St Luke

Every year Joseph and Mary went to Jerusalem to celebrate the Jewish Passover. When Jesus was 12 years old, he made the journey with them.

After the feast, Mary and Joseph set off for home, but that evening, when they realised that Jesus was missing, they returned to Jerusalem to look for him. After searching for three days, they finally found Jesus in the Temple. He was sitting with the Jewish teachers, listening to them and asking them questions, and they were filled with admiration for him.

Mary and Joseph were astonished when they saw him and said, 'Son, we have been so worried for three days! Why have you done this to us?'

Jesus answered, 'Why were you looking for me? Did you not realise that I would be in my Father's house?' But they did not understand what his answer meant.

The family returned to Nazareth, and Mary kept all these things in her heart. Jesus grew in height and wisdom, and was loved by God and all who knew him.

This is the Gospel of the Lord
**Praise to you, Lord Jesus Christ**

# Second Sunday after Christmas

*John 1:1-18*

A reading from the Gospel of St John.

When everything first began, the Word already existed. The Word was with God; and the Word was God. From the very beginning, all things were created through him. All life came from the Word, and this life was the light for all people. The light shines out in the darkness, and the darkness could never conquer it.

God sent a man called John, to be a witness for the light, so that others would believe because of him, even though he was not the light. The real light was the Word who was coming into the world to give light to everyone.

He was in the world created through him, and yet the world did not know him. He came to his own people and they did not accept him. To those who did receive him he gave the right to become children of God, the offspring of God himself.

The Word became flesh and he lived as a man among us. We saw his glory given by the Father to his only Son, full of grace and truth.

John, as his witness, told the world: 'This is the one I spoke about when I said: "He comes after me but is greater than I am because he already existed before I was born." From him we have received many graces, for while God gave the Law through Moses, we receive his grace and truth through Jesus Christ. No one has ever seen God, but his only Son, who is nearest to his Father's heart, has made him known to us.'

This is the Gospel of the Lord
**Praise to you, Lord Jesus Christ**

# THE EPIPHANY OF THE LORD

*Matthew 2:1-12*

A reading from the Gospel of St Matthew

Jesus was born in Bethlehem, a small town in Judaea when King Herod ruled the land. Some wise men from the east travelled to Jerusalem and asked King Herod where they could find the new-born King of the Jews whom they had come to worship.

Herod was greatly troubled because he didn't want anyone else to be king, so he sent for his advisers. 'Tell me where this child, the so-called King, will be born,' he said.

'It has been foretold by the prophets that he will be born in Bethlehem,' they answered.

For the prophets had written:
>And you, Bethlehem in Judaea,
>are not the least important among Judaean cities,
>for from you a leader will come,
>a shepherd for my people Israel!

King Herod sent for the wise men privately, and asked them to tell him exactly when the star had first appeared. Then he said to them, 'I will allow you to search for this child, but you must come back and tell me where to find him. Then I too can go and honour him.'

The wise men set off again on their journey. They followed the bright star until it appeared to stop over a house, where they found Mary with the baby Jesus. They were filled with wonder and joy, and, falling to their knees to worship him, they gave him gifts of gold, frankincense and myrrh.

An angel warned them in a dream not to return to Herod's palace, so they went back to their own country a different way.

This is the Gospel of the Lord
**Praise to you, Lord Jesus Christ**

# THE BAPTISM OF THE LORD

*Luke 3:15-16, 21-22*

A reading from the Gospel of St Luke

The people grew excited and many began to think that John might be the Messiah promised by God, so John told them, 'I baptise you with water, but someone is coming who will baptise you with the Holy Spirit. He is filled with God's power and I am unfit to undo his sandals.'

After Jesus had been baptised by John, the heavens opened and the Holy Spirit appeared as a dove and settled on Jesus. Then a voice from heaven said, 'You are my Son; my favour rests on you.'

This is the Gospel of the Lord
**Praise to you, Lord Jesus Christ**

# First Sunday of Lent

*Luke 4:1-13*

A reading from the Gospel of St Luke

Jesus was filled with the Holy Spirit which led him into the desert where he was tempted by the devil for forty days. All that time he had nothing to eat and he was famished.

The devil said to him, 'If you are God's Son, then turn this stone into a tasty loaf of bread.'

Jesus replied, 'Scripture tells us that man does not live on bread alone.'

Then the devil tempted Jesus a second time by showing him a glimpse of all the kingdoms of the world. 'All this belongs to me,' he said, 'but I will give this power and glory to you if you worship me!'

Jesus answered him, 'Scripture tells us to worship the Lord our God and serve him alone.'

Then the devil led Jesus to the Temple in Jerusalem, and on its rooftop he tempted him for a third time. 'If you are indeed the Son of God,' the devil said, 'then throw yourself off, for Scripture says: God has ordered his angels to guard you and they will cradle you in their arms to protect you from any harm.'

Jesus said to the devil, 'Scripture also tells us: do not put the Lord God to the test.'

Finally, the devil gave up trying to tempt Jesus, and he left him alone and waited for his next opportunity.

This is the Gospel of the Lord
**Praise to you, Lord Jesus Christ**

## Second Sunday of Lent

*Luke 9:28-36*

A reading from the Gospel of St Luke

With the disciples Peter, James and John, Jesus climbed a mountain to pray. While Jesus prayed, his clothes shone with dazzling white light as radiant as the sun, and his appearance was transformed!

Suddenly, Moses and Elijah appeared in glory next to Jesus and began speaking to him.

Peter and his friends were amazed by everything they saw, and Peter said to Jesus, 'Lord, this is all so wonderful! I could build three shelters, one for each of you!'

At that moment a cloud descended and covered them on the mountain top, and the disciples were afraid. Then a voice from the cloud spoke, 'This is my Son, the chosen one, listen to what he says.'

When the voice fell silent, the disciples found themselves alone with Jesus. The three friends told no one at that time about the wonders they had witnessed that day.

This is the Gospel of the Lord
**Praise to you, Lord Jesus Christ**

# Third Sunday of Lent

*Luke 13:1-9*

A reading from the Gospel of St Luke

Some of the people told Jesus about the Galileans who had been killed by Pilate while offering sacrifices to God.

Jesus said to them, 'Just because they were killed doesn't mean that they were worse sinners than anyone else. Think of the eighteen people in Siloam who died when the tower fell on them. Do you think that proves that they were guiltier than anyone else in Jerusalem? Indeed, it does not! And I tell you that you will all come to the same end unless you turn away from your sins.'

Then he told them a parable:

A man went to check how many fruits were growing on a fig tree in his vineyard, but he found there was none. So he sent for his gardener and told him, 'This tree has grown no fruit for the last three years. Cut it down and make space for another.'

But the gardener said to him, 'Master, give the tree one more year so I have time to feed and care for it. If it still has no fruit on it, then cut it down.'

This is the Gospel of the Lord
**Praise to you, Lord Jesus Christ**

HEAR THE GOOD NEWS

# Fourth Sunday of Lent

*Luke 15:1-3, 11-32*

A reading from the Gospel of St Luke

A crowd of tax collectors and other sinners had gathered around Jesus, much to the anger and disdain of the scribes and Pharisees. When Jesus overheard them complaining, he told them a parable:

> There was a man who had two sons and the younger one came to his father and said, 'Father, give me everything that will one day belong to me, so I can enjoy my riches now.'
>
> The father did this, and the son set off to look for adventure. He travelled to a distant land and spent all his money enjoying himself.
>
> There was a famine in that land, and the young man found himself penniless and hungry. 'If I stay here I will surely starve,' he thought, so he decided to return to his father and ask for his forgiveness.
>
> The father saw his son coming and ran to welcome him. As he hugged him, the young man said, 'Father, I am so sorry. I no longer deserve to be called your son.'
>
> But the father told his servants to prepare a feast and to bring the finest clothes, and they began to celebrate.
>
> When the man's other son returned home from working in the fields, he asked the servants, 'What is the reason for such a celebration?'
>
> When he heard their explanation, he was filled

with anger and refused to join the party. So his father came looking for him, and the son said to him, 'I have been hard-working and loyal, and never once did you throw such a party for me. Yet you are happy to do so for my brother who has been greedy and selfish and treated you very badly.'

The father answered his son, 'You are always with me, and everything I have belongs to you. Your brother who was lost has been found. He is not dead after all, but alive, and it is only right that we should celebrate his return with joy!'

This is the Gospel of the Lord
**Praise to you, Lord Jesus Christ**

# Fifth Sunday of Lent

*John 8:1-11*

A reading from the Gospel of St John

Jesus was teaching in the Temple when the Pharisees brought a woman to stand before him. 'This woman has been caught doing something wrong, and the law says that she should be stoned. What do you think?' they asked, because they wanted to trick Jesus.

After a few moments Jesus stood up and said, 'Let the person who has never done anything wrong throw the first stone at her.'

The crowd that had gathered began to leave one by one, until Jesus and the woman stood alone. Jesus said to her, 'Has anyone thrown a stone at you?'

'No, sir,' she answered.

'Then I have forgiven you,' he said. 'Now go and sin no more.'

This is the Gospel of the Lord
**Praise to you, Lord Jesus Christ**

YEAR C

# PALM (PASSION) SUNDAY – LITURGY OF THE PALMS

*Luke 19:28-40*

A reading from the Gospel of St Luke

Jesus made his way to Jerusalem, and when he reached the Mount of Olives, he sent two of his disciples to fetch a young colt from a nearby village.

'If anyone asks, tell them that the master needs it,' Jesus said, and they did as he had explained.

They brought the colt to Jesus, and laid a cloak on it, before helping him on to its back.

Crowds of people had lined the road to Jerusalem, and were waiting to welcome Jesus when he came. As he approached, they threw cloaks on the road before him and sang out in greeting: 'Blessed is the King who comes in the Lord's name! Peace and glory in the highest heavens!'

Hearing this, some of the Pharisees urged Jesus to quieten the crowd, but Jesus said to them, 'The very stones will cry out if their voices are silenced.'

This is the Gospel of the Lord
**Praise to you, Lord Jesus Christ**

# Palm (Passion) Sunday – Liturgy of the Passion

*Longer version – Luke 22:14-23:56*

A reading from the Gospel of St Luke

Jesus and his apostles were sitting at table together when he said to them, 'I have wanted so much to share this Passover with you before I suffer; now you shall know that I will not eat it again until it is fulfilled in God's kingdom.'

Then he took a cup and gave thanks to God, and said, 'Take this and share it with each other, for I shall not drink wine again until the kingdom of God comes.'

Afterwards he took some bread, and gave thanks to God before he broke it and shared it with them, saying, 'This is my body, given for you. Do this to remember me.'

After supper, he gave them a cup of wine in the same way, saying, 'This cup is a new covenant with God, a promise sealed with my blood which will be poured out for you!'

Then Jesus told the disciples, 'I tell you now that my betrayer shares this very table with me. Indeed, the Son of Man will suffer and die according to God's plan, but how dreadful for the man responsible for that betrayal!'

At once the disciples began to talk among themselves about which of them could possibly do such a thing.

When an argument broke out later about which of them was the greatest, Jesus told them, 'Kings have power over their subjects, but you must not act this way. The one who is greatest must be like the youngest and least important, and whoever leads you must be like a servant. Which is the more important: the person who sits to eat or the one who serves them? Of course it is the one sitting down to eat! Yet I have come to serve rather than be served. My friends, you have been loyal and stood by me faithfully. So, just as my father gave me a kingdom, now I give one to you. You will share food and drink with me in my kingdom, and each of you will have a place in heaven.'

Then Jesus turned to Simon Peter and said, 'Simon, Simon! The devil wants to test you, to separate the wheat from the chaff, and I have prayed that your faith will not let you down. When you have recovered, you must be ready in turn to give strength to your brothers.'

Simon Peter answered Jesus, 'Lord, I am ready to go to prison and even to die for you!'

Jesus replied sadly, 'Peter, by the time the cock crows, you will have said three times that you do not know me.'

Jesus turned to his disciples and asked, 'Did you need anything when I sent you out without purse, bags, or sandals?'

'Not a thing,' they replied.

'Now,' Jesus said, 'you must take a purse or bag if you have one, and if you have no sword, sell your coat to buy one. Because the words of Scripture which say, "He was treated like a criminal", are coming true about me.'

The disciples said to him, 'Lord, we have two swords!'

And Jesus replied, 'That will do.'

After supper Jesus set off with his disciples for the Mount of Olives. When they arrived, Jesus told them, 'Pray that you are not put to the test.'

Then he moved a short distance from them and began to pray. 'Father,' he implored, 'if it is possible, take this suffering away from me. If not, let your will, and not mine, be done.' And an angel from heaven appeared to give him strength.

In his torment, Jesus prayed even harder, and his sweat fell to the ground like drops of blood. When he rose from his prayer and returned to the disciples, he found them asleep, exhausted by their sadness. He woke them, saying, 'Why are you sleeping? Get up and pray that you are not tested.'

Even as he spoke, a crowd appeared, led by the disciple Judas. Walking up to Jesus, he went to kiss him but Jesus said to him, 'Will you betray the Son of Man with a kiss?'

When his disciples realised what was happening they shouted to Jesus, 'Lord, shall we use our sword?'

At that moment, one of them struck out and cut an ear off the high priest's servant. So Jesus stopped them, saying, 'Enough, no more!' And he reached out and healed the man's ear.

Turning to the chief priests and the guards they had brought with them, Jesus asked, 'Am I a criminal? Why else do you come with swords and weapons? Day after day in the Temple you made no attempt to arrest me, and now you act secretly under the cover of darkness.'

After his arrest Jesus was taken to the house of the high priest where Peter followed him at a distance. In the courtyard some people sat warming themselves by a fire, and Peter went and sat among them. One of the servant girls recognised Peter and said, 'This man was with Jesus!' But Peter denied that he knew Jesus.

Later Peter was recognised again, and once more he denied Jesus, saying, 'I am not one of them.'

A short time passed before yet another man noticed Peter and said, 'This man was definitely with Jesus!'

Peter insisted, 'I have no idea what you are talking about!'

At that moment a cock crowed, and Jesus turned and looked straight at Peter. Remembering what Jesus had told him only hours before, Peter realised what he had done and went outside to weep. Meanwhile Jesus was mocked and teased by the guards who insulted and beat him.

When morning came, Jesus was brought before the council of elders, and the chief priests and scribes, to answer their questions. 'Tell us if you are the Christ, the promised Messiah,' they said.

Jesus replied, 'You will not believe me if I tell you. The Son of Man will sit at almighty God's right hand from now on'.

'So you are indeed the Son of God,' they said.

Jesus replied, 'You are the ones who say I am.'

The council erupted in uproar. 'We have heard it from his own lips, we need no other proof,' they said, and they took Jesus before Pilate.

The council appeared with Jesus and began to tell Pilate their accusations against him. 'This man is misleading our people,' they said, 'encouraging them to rebel, and not to pay taxes to Caesar. He claims to be the Messiah, a king!'

Pilate put a question to Jesus: 'Are you indeed the King of the Jews?'

Jesus answered, 'Those are your words.'

Pilate could find no fault in Jesus, but the council insisted, 'This man's teaching is causing trouble all over Judaea, all the way from Galilee to Jerusalem!' Then realising that Jesus was from Galilee, Pilate sent him before Herod who had authority over that region.

Herod was pleased to have an opportunity at last to meet Jesus. He had heard many amazing things about him and hoped that he might perform a miracle. Herod questioned Jesus for a long time, but could get no answer from him, and all the while the chief priests and council members continued their forceful accusations against him.

Finally Herod grew impatient, and he and his soldiers taunted Jesus scornfully before wrapping a cloak around him and sending him back to Pilate. From that day Herod and Pilate were no longer enemies, but allies.

Pilate called the chief priests and leaders of the people together. 'You have brought this man before me as a troublemaker,' he said, 'but neither Herod nor I can find him guilty of any crime. He does not deserve to die, but I will have him flogged and then set him free.'

But with one voice they shouted, 'Take him and set Barabbas free!' (Barabbas was a murderer who had caused a riot in the city.)

Pilate argued against them because he wanted to free Jesus, but they shouted only louder, 'Crucify him!'

Again Pilate objected, 'Why kill him when he has done nothing wrong?'

The shouts of the crowd grew louder and louder as they called for Jesus to be crucified. Finally, fearing a riot, Pilate agreed to their demands and ordered Barabbas to be released while Jesus was handed over, for them to do what they wished.

As the soldiers led Jesus away, they met a man from Cyrene, called Simon, and forced him to carry the cross behind Jesus.

A great crowd of people followed Jesus, many of whom were women who wept for him. Jesus said to them, 'Women of Jerusalem, do not be sad for me, but for yourselves and your children. A time will come when people will be glad that they have no children. They will say to the mountains, "Fall on us", and beg the hills to cover them. For if things such as these happen when the wood is green, what will happen when the wood is dry?'

Two others were led out to be put to death with Jesus, and when they reached the place called the skull, they were crucified, one on his right and the other on his left.

Jesus prayed, 'Father, forgive them, for they do not understand what they are doing.'

While they threw dice to divide his clothes between them, some of the crowd jeered: 'If he is God's chosen one let him save himself; he's saved others!'

Even the soldiers mocked him, 'If you are King of the Jews, save yourself,' they called, and they hung a sign above him which read, 'This is the King of the Jews.'

One of the criminals hanging next to Jesus taunted him by saying, 'Aren't you the Christ? Can't you save yourself and us as well?'

But the other criminal scolded the first. 'Have you no fear of God?' he said. 'We deserve this punishment! We are paying for our crimes, but this man has done nothing wrong.' Then, turning to Jesus, he said, 'Jesus, when you come into your kingdom remember me.'

Jesus answered him, 'This very day I promise that you will be with me in paradise.'

Then about the sixth hour darkness fell upon the land, until the ninth hour, when the curtain hanging in the temple was torn in two.

In a loud voice Jesus cried out, 'Father, I place my spirit in your hands!' And then he died.

The Centurion standing close to Jesus had seen everything that had happened and said aloud, 'Truly, this was a good man.'

The crowd which had gathered to watch Jesus die went away filled with sorrow. The friends of Jesus and the women who had followed him stood a short distance away and saw everything that took place.

Joseph of Arimathaea, a friend of Jesus and a member of the council of leaders, went to Pilate and asked for the body. He took Jesus down from the cross, wrapped him in linen cloths and laid him in an unused tomb cut from stone.

The women followed Joseph to the tomb and saw where Jesus was laid. Then they went away to prepare spices and perfumes for his burial, but the next day they rested because it was the Sabbath.

This is the Gospel of the Lord
**Praise to you, Lord Jesus Christ**

# Palm (Passion) Sunday – Liturgy of the Passion

*Shorter version – Luke 23:1-49*

A reading from the Gospel of St Luke

The council appeared with Jesus and began to tell Pilate their accusations against him. 'This man is misleading our people,' they said, 'encouraging them to rebel, and not to pay taxes to Caesar. He claims to be the Messiah, a king!'

Pilate put a question to Jesus:, 'Are you indeed the King of the Jews?'

Jesus answered, 'Those are your words.'

Pilate could find no fault in Jesus, but the council insisted, 'This man's teaching is causing trouble all over Judaea, all the way from Galilee to Jerusalem!' Then realising that Jesus was from Galilee, Pilate sent him before Herod who had authority over that region.

Herod was pleased to have an opportunity at last to meet Jesus. He had heard many amazing things about him and hoped that he might perform a miracle. Herod questioned Jesus for a long time, but could get no answer from him, and all the while the chief priests and council members continued their forceful accusations against him.

Finally Herod grew impatient, and he and his soldiers taunted Jesus scornfully before wrapping a cloak around him and sending him back to Pilate. From that day Herod and Pilate were no longer enemies, but allies.

Pilate called the chief priests and leaders of the

people together. 'You have brought this man before me as a troublemaker,' he said, 'but neither Herod nor I can find him guilty of any crime. He does not deserve to die, but I will have him flogged and then set him free.'

But with one voice they shouted, 'Take him and set Barabbas free!' (Barabbas was a murderer who had caused a riot in the city.)

Pilate argued against them because he wanted to free Jesus, but they shouted only louder, 'Crucify him!'

Again Pilate objected, 'Why kill him when he has done nothing wrong?'

The shouts of the crowd grew louder and louder as they called for Jesus to be crucified. Finally, fearing a riot, Pilate agreed to their demands and ordered Barabbas to be released, while Jesus was handed over for them to do what they wished.

As the soldiers led Jesus away, they met a man from Cyrene, called Simon, and forced him to carry the cross behind Jesus.

A great crowd of people followed Jesus, many of whom were women who wept for him. Jesus said to them, 'Women of Jerusalem, do not be sad for me, but for yourselves and your children. A time will come when people will be glad that they have no children. They will say to the mountains, "Fall on us", and beg the hills to cover them. For if things such as these happen when the wood is green, what will happen when the wood is dry?'

Two others were led out to be put to death with Jesus, and when they reached the place called the skull, they were crucified, one on his right and the other on his left.

Jesus prayed, 'Father, forgive them, for they do not understand what they are doing.'

While they threw dice to divide his clothes between them, some of the crowd jeered: 'If he is God's chosen one let him save himself; he's saved others!'

Even the soldiers mocked him, 'If you are King of the Jews, save yourself,' they called, and they hung a sign above him which read, 'This is the King of the Jews.'

One of the criminals hanging next to Jesus taunted him by saying, 'Aren't you the Christ? Can't you save yourself and us as well?'

But the other criminal scolded the first. 'Have you no fear of God?' he said. 'We deserve this punishment! We are paying for our crimes, but this man has done nothing wrong.' Then, turning to Jesus, he said, 'Jesus, when you come into your kingdom remember me.'

Jesus answered him, 'This very day I promise that you will be with me in paradise.'

Then about the sixth hour darkness fell upon the land, until the ninth hour, when the curtain hanging in the temple was torn in two.

In a loud voice Jesus cried out, 'Father, I place my spirit in your hands!' And then he died.

The Centurion standing close to Jesus had seen everything that had happened and said aloud, 'Truly, this was a good man.'

The crowd which had gathered to watch Jesus die went away filled with sorrow. The friends of Jesus and the women who had followed him stood a short distance away and saw everything that took place.

This is the Gospel of the Lord
**Praise to you, Lord Jesus Christ**

# Easter Day

*John 20:1-9*

A reading from the Gospel of St John

Very early on the Sunday morning Mary of Magdala went to the tomb where Jesus had been laid. Seeing that the stone had been rolled back from the entrance to the tomb, Mary ran to find Peter and John.

'They have taken the Lord,' she cried, 'and I don't know where they have put him!'

The apostles ran to the tomb, and John, arriving first, saw the cloths lying on the ground. When Peter reached the tomb, he went in and he too saw the cloths that had once been wrapped around the body of Jesus.

Standing together, John and Peter understood for the first time what the Scriptures had meant about Christ rising from the dead.

This is the Gospel of the Lord
**Praise to you, Lord Jesus Christ**

# Easter Day

*Alternative reading – Luke 24:1-12*

A reading from the Gospel of St Luke

At sunrise on the Sunday morning some of the women took the burial spices they had prepared and went to the tomb where Jesus had been laid.

To their surprise they found that the stone had been rolled away from the entrance to the tomb, and the body of Jesus was gone.

As they stood wondering what had happened, two angels appeared next to them and asked, 'Why do you look for the living among the dead? Remember how he told you that he would rise again on the third day. He is not here because he is risen!'

As they recalled the words of Jesus, the women ran to find the apostles to tell them everything that had happened. The apostles listened to the women but could not believe what they heard, so Peter decided to run to the tomb to see for himself. He found everything just as the women had described, and, full of amazement, he returned to tell the others what he had seen.

This is the Gospel of the Lord
**Praise to you, Lord Jesus Christ**

# SECOND SUNDAY OF EASTER

*John 20:19-31*

A reading from the Gospel of St John

On the Sunday after Jesus had died his disciples sat huddled together in a locked room, hidden away for fear of being arrested.

Suddenly Jesus appeared in the room with them. 'Peace be with you,' he said and he showed them the wounds in his hands and his side. The disciples were overjoyed to see their master again.

'As my Father sent me, so I am sending you,' said Jesus. Then, breathing on them, he said, 'Receive the Holy Spirit, and know that whoever you forgive I will forgive also!'

The disciple called Thomas was not with the others when Jesus had appeared, and because he had not seen him with his own eyes, he did not believe that Jesus was alive.

A week later Jesus appeared to them again and greeted them with the words, 'Peace be with you.' He showed his wounds to Thomas and said, 'Doubt no longer, Thomas.'

At once Thomas fell to his knees and cried, 'My Lord and my God.'

Jesus said to him, 'You believe because you have seen me with your own eyes. Blessed are those who have not seen and yet believe.'

Jesus performed many other miracles which his disciples witnessed, but they are not written down in this book. The ones recorded here have been written so you may believe that Jesus is the Son of God, and through this belief you may have everlasting life.

This is the Gospel of the Lord
**Praise to you, Lord Jesus Christ**

# Third Sunday of Easter

*John 21:1-19*

A reading from the Gospel of St John

Jesus appeared again to his disciples by the sea of Tiberius. Simon Peter and some of the disciples had been fishing all night but had caught nothing. As daylight dawned Jesus stood on the shore, although they did not recognise him, and he asked them, 'Have you caught anything?' As they shook their heads in reply, he said to them, 'Try once more over there, and you will catch something!'

They threw their nets back into the water and caught so many fish that their nets were ready to burst. As soon as Simon Peter recognised Jesus, he jumped into the water and swam to meet him.

On the beach Jesus had made a fire and was cooking breakfast for his friends, and they shared a meal together of bread and fresh fish.

When they had finished eating, Jesus turned to Peter and asked, 'Do you love me more than anyone?'

'Yes, Lord, you know that I love you,' Peter replied.

'Then feed my lambs,' Jesus said.

Again Jesus put the same question to Peter, and again Peter gave the same reply: 'Lord, you know I love you.'

Jesus said to him, 'Take care of my sheep.'

When Jesus asked Peter the same question for a third time, Peter felt sad and hurt, and he said to Jesus, 'Lord, you know everything, so you must know how much I love you!'

Again Jesus said to Peter, 'Take care of my sheep.' He told Peter how he would give glory to God, and then he said to him, 'Come, follow me.'

This is the Gospel of the Lord
**Praise to you, Lord Jesus Christ**

# Fourth Sunday of Easter

*John 10:27-30*

A reading from the Gospel of St John

Jesus said:

My sheep know my voice and they follow me as I lead them to everlasting life. I know each one of them by name, and they can always trust me to take care of them and to protect them from harm. No one can steal them away from my Father's care, and the Father and I are one.

This is the Gospel of the Lord
**Praise to you, Lord Jesus Christ**

# Fifth Sunday of Easter

*John 13:31-35*

A reading from the Gospel of St John

When Judas had left them, Jesus turned to his apostles and said:

Now God's glory is revealed through the Son. It will soon be time for me to leave you, my friends, and you cannot come where I am going. So I give you a new commandment: I want you to love each other as I have loved each one of you. If you live by this rule, other people will see your goodness and love, and they will know that you are my disciples.

This is the Gospel of the Lord
**Praise to you, Lord Jesus Christ**

# Sixth Sunday of Easter

*John 14:23-29*

A reading from the Gospel of St John

Jesus said:

Whoever loves me will keep my word, and my Father and I will live in them and love them. If they have no love for me, then neither will they love my word. Everything I tell you comes from my heavenly Father.

I have told you all these things while I have been with you, but my Father will send the Holy Spirit in my name. The Spirit will help you to remember my word and teach you all that you need to know. I give you the gift of my own peace, which cannot come from the world, so that you will not feel afraid or troubled. I have told you that I am leaving, and I shall return. Because you love me, be glad that I am going to my Father. I have told you all this now, so that when it happens you will understand and believe.

This is the Gospel of the Lord
**Praise to you, Lord Jesus Christ**

# THE ASCENSION OF THE LORD

*Luke 24:46-53*

A reading from the Gospel of St John

Jesus said to his disciples:

> So it is written that the Christ would suffer and rise again on the third day, and in his name repentance and the forgiveness of sins would be preached to people everywhere. You, my friends, are witnesses to all this. I will send you what has been promised by my Father, but wait in Jerusalem until that time when God's power will come to you.

Jesus then led them to Bethany where he left them and was taken up to heaven. Filled with joy, the disciples returned to Jerusalem and spent their time praising God in the Temple.

This is the Gospel of the Lord
**Praise to you, Lord Jesus Christ**

## SEVENTH SUNDAY OF EASTER

*John 17:20-26*

A reading from the Gospel of St John

Looking up to heaven, Jesus prayed:

Heavenly Father, take care of my disciples and everyone who comes to believe in you because of them. Unite them in love and make them one, just as you and I are one. Father, just as you are in me, and I am in you, may they be in us so that the world will believe that you sent me, and that you love them just as you love me.

This is the Gospel of the Lord
**Praise to you, Lord Jesus Christ**

# PENTECOST SUNDAY

*First reading – Acts 2:1-11*

A reading from the Acts of the Apostles

The disciples had gathered together in Jerusalem to celebrate the Feast of Pentecost and to wait for the Holy Spirit that Jesus had promised to send.

One day, as they were praying together, the room was suddenly filled with the sound of a powerful wind which roared through the house. Then, what looked like small tongues of fire appeared and spread out to touch each one of them. So it was that they were filled with the Holy Spirit.

At once, in their excitement, they rushed outside to tell everyone what had happened to them. As they began to speak, they were amazed to find that everyone listening to their words could understand them! People from different regions and countries were astounded to hear these men preaching to them in their own native languages.

This is the Word of the Lord
**Thanks be to God**

# PENTECOST SUNDAY

*Gospel – John 14:15-16, 23-26*

A reading from the Gospel of St John

Jesus said:

If you love me you will do everything I have commanded, and I will ask my Father to send a helper to stay with you for ever. Anyone who keeps my word, which comes from the Father who sent me, will be loved by my Father and me, and we will make our home in their hearts. The Spirit of God will show you the truth and live inside you. This Spirit will teach you and help you to remember everything I have told you.

This is the Gospel of the Lord
**Praise to you, Lord Jesus Christ**

# Trinity Sunday

*John 16:12-15*

A reading from the Gospel of St John

Jesus said to his disciples:

> My friends, there is so much more to tell you, but I will not burden you now. Do not worry; when the Spirit of truth comes he will guide you to the complete truth and reveal the things to come. He will glorify me, because everything he says will come from me, and everything that is mine comes from the Father.

This is the Gospel of the Lord
**Praise to you, Lord Jesus Christ**

# Second Sunday of the Year

*John 2:1-11*

A reading from the Gospel of St John

Jesus and his mother, together with his disciples, were invited to a wedding in a town called Cana. There was food to eat and wine to drink, and the celebrations carried on throughout the evening.

Then Mary came to Jesus and said, 'Son, there is no more wine for the guests to drink.'

'Why do you ask for help when my time has not yet come?' Jesus asked.

But Mary turned to the servants and said to them, 'Do whatever Jesus tells you.'

Nearby stood six very large water jars, and Jesus told the servants to fill them with water. 'Now pour some out and take it to the head waiter,' he said.

The water had been changed to wine, and when he had tasted it the head waiter went to the bridegroom and said, 'Sir, you have certainly saved the very best wine until last!'

This was the first miracle Jesus performed and it happened at Cana in Galilee. His disciples had witnessed his glory and they believed in him.

This is the Gospel of the Lord
**Praise to you, Lord Jesus Christ**

# Third Sunday of the Year

*Luke 1:1-4; 4:14-21*

A reading from the Gospel of St Luke

Like others before me, I have decided to recount the events and words which have been passed on to us by those who witnessed them with their own eyes and ears, so that you, Theophilus, might understand where the knowledge of our teaching comes from.

Filled with the Holy Spirit, Jesus returned to Galilee, and wherever he taught in the synagogues he was praised by everyone who heard him speak. Soon his name was known far and wide throughout the countryside. Jesus came to Nazareth, the town where he had spent his childhood, and on the Sabbath day he went to the synagogue. He unrolled the scroll and began to read the words of the prophet Isaiah:

> The Lord's Spirit has been given to me.
> He has sent me to bring the Good News to the poor,
> to declare freedom for prisoners,
> to give new sight to the blind,
> to set the downtrodden free.

When Jesus had finished, he rolled up the scroll and sat down. The synagogue was hushed and still, as everyone there watched him carefully. Looking up, Jesus said to them, 'These words you have heard today are coming true, even as I speak.'

This is the Gospel of the Lord
**Praise to you, Lord Jesus Christ**

# Fourth Sunday of the Year

*Luke 4:21-30*

A reading from the Gospel of St Luke

Looking up from what he had been reading in the synagogue, Jesus said to the people, 'These words you have heard today are coming true, even as I speak.'

The people were amazed by all that he said. Some of them began to ask, 'Isn't this the Son of Joseph the carpenter?'

Jesus replied, 'No prophet is ever accepted by his own people, and doubtless you will expect me to do here what I have done for people elsewhere. In Elijah's day, when a great famine struck he was not sent to help the widows of Israel but to help a widow in Sidon. In the same way, the prophet Elisha cured Naaman the Syrian rather than the Israelites suffering in the same way.'

Infuriated by his words, the people took Jesus to a hilltop outside the town, intent on throwing him off, but he managed to make his escape without coming to any harm.

This is the Gospel of the Lord
**Praise to you, Lord Jesus Christ**

# Fifth Sunday of the Year

*Luke 5:1-11*

A reading from the Gospel of St Luke

Jesus was preaching by the Sea of Galilee, when crowds of people gathered all around to listen to him. Jesus noticed two fishing boats tied up nearby, so he climbed aboard one, which belonged to Peter, and asked him to sail a little way from the shore.

When Jesus had finished talking to the crowds, he turned to Peter and said, 'Sail out to the deep water and cast out your nets.'

'Master, we have been fishing all night and have caught nothing,' Peter said, 'but I will do whatever you say.'

That day they caught so many fish that their nets were ready to burst. Peter and his friends James and John were filled with wonder by this marvellous sight and fell to their knees.

Then Jesus said, 'Do not be afraid; come and follow me.'

So they left their boats and became his disciples.

This is the Gospel of the Lord
**Praise to you, Lord Jesus Christ**

## Sixth Sunday of the Year

*Luke 6:17, 20-26*

A reading from the Gospel of St Luke

Jesus and his twelve disciples stopped at a level plain where crowds of people had gathered. The crowds had come from all over Judaea and as far as the coastal regions of Tyre and Sidon.

Jesus looked at his disciples and said:

> Happy are you who are poor: the kingdom of God belongs to you.
> Happy are you who go hungry: you shall be satisfied.
> Happy are you who weep with sadness: you shall laugh.
> Happy are you who suffer hatred and abuse because of the Son of Man: give thanks and dance for joy, because a great reward awaits you in heaven.
> The prophets were treated in just the same way by their forebears before them.
> But how terrible for you who are rich: you have had your time of comfort.
> How terrible for you who are well fed now: you shall be hungry.
> How terrible for you who are laughing now: you shall know sadness and tears.
> How terrible if people speak kindly of you!
> Their ancestors said the same about the false prophets.

This is the Gospel of the Lord
**Praise to you, Lord Jesus Christ**

YEAR C

# Seventh Sunday of the Year

*Luke 6:27-38*

A reading from the Gospel of St Luke

Jesus said:

Love your enemies, and treat those who hate you with kindness; bless those who curse you, pray for those who are cruel to you. When someone hits you on one cheek, offer the other one too; when someone takes your coat, give them your shirt as well. Give to everyone who asks, and when someone takes what belongs to you do not ask them to return it. Treat other people just as you would like them to treat you.

It is easy to love those who love you, and to treat kind people with kindness in return, so what merit can you expect? Even sinners do the same! They too will lend to others if they know that they will be repaid in full. You must love your enemies and do good without expecting anything in return. You will be children of God and receive great reward for your goodness.

Show mercy to others just as your Father shows mercy to you. If you do not judge others, God will not judge you. Do not look for guilt in others and God will not look for your guilt; if you are forgiving, then God will show you forgiveness too; if you give generously to others, then God will pour out his gifts generously for you, because whatever you measure out for others will be measured out for you!

This is the Gospel of the Lord
**Praise to you, Lord Jesus Christ**

# Eighth Sunday of the Year

*Luke 6:39-45*

A reading from the Gospel of St Luke

Jesus said to the people:

> Can one blind person lead another safely without both coming to harm? A disciple can learn to become as good as the teacher who trains them, but not better. Why do you notice the splinter in someone else's eye, but do not see the log in your own? You cannot offer to remove the splinter until you have removed the log from your own eye first. Only then will you be able to see clearly enough to do so.

> Just as fruit that is rotten and bad can never grow on a strong and healthy tree, so good fruit cannot grow on a tree that is sick and diseased. Different fruits grow on different trees, and everyone knows which fruit belongs to which type of tree. In the same way, a person's actions and words flow from what is in their hearts. Goodness will flow from what is good, and wickedness from what is bad.

This is the Gospel of the Lord
**Praise to you, Lord Jesus Christ**

# NINTH SUNDAY OF THE YEAR

*Luke 7:1-10*

A reading from the Gospel of St Luke

While Jesus was in Capernaum, some of the Jews came to him to ask for help. They had been sent by a Roman centurion whose favourite servant was very ill and close to death. 'Jesus, please help this man, because he has always been fair and kind to us,' they said.

Jesus went with them, but on the way they were met by some of the centurion's friends with a message for Jesus from the centurion which said, 'Jesus, do not put yourself to any trouble for my sake, because I am not good enough to expect you to come to me. I am a soldier, and I obey my orders just as my men obey me. Whatever I tell them to do, they will do it. If you will just give the order, I know that my servant will be well again.'

Jesus was amazed by the centurion's faith in his power, and said, 'Few people have shown such great trust in me.'

When the centurion's friends returned to his house they found great rejoicing because the servant had completely recovered.

This is the Gospel of the Lord
**Praise to you, Lord Jesus Christ**

# Tenth Sunday of the Year

*Luke 7:11-17*

A reading from the Gospel of St Luke

A large crowd had followed Jesus and his disciples to a town called Nain, where they met a funeral procession outside the gates of the town. A widow's only son had died, and she walked behind the procession crying sadly.

Jesus was filled with great pity and said to the woman, 'Do not cry.' Then he stopped the procession and said loudly, 'Young man, get up!'

At once the young man sat up and began to talk, and Jesus brought him to his mother.

The woman and the crowd were filled with wonder and began to praise God, and soon everyone had heard about the marvellous thing which Jesus had done.

This is the Gospel of the Lord
**Praise to you, Lord Jesus Christ**

# Eleventh Sunday of the Year

*Luke 7:36-8:3*

A reading from the Gospel of St Luke

One of the Pharisees called Simon invited Jesus to dinner. A woman who had done many things she was ashamed of heard that Jesus would be there and came to find him. She knelt at his feet and began to cry, wiping his feet dry with her long hair before covering them with kisses and perfumed ointment.

Simon was annoyed that Jesus would allow such a person near him. But Jesus knew what Simon was thinking and asked him, 'If one servant owed his master fifty pounds and another owed his master five thousand pounds, which one would love his master more if the debts were cancelled?'

'The one who owed more,' Simon answered.

Then Jesus said, 'Simon, you did not offer me water to wash with, a kiss as a greeting, or perfume to refresh me. This woman has done all these things and more. Surely everything she has done wrong has been forgiven for her to show such great love. Where little has been forgiven, little love is shown.'

The other dinner guests wondered who this Jesus was, that he could forgive the sins of others.

Then Jesus said to the woman, 'Your faith has saved you! Go now, your sins have been forgiven.'

This is the Gospel of the Lord
**Praise to you, Lord Jesus Christ**

## Twelfth Sunday of the Year

*Luke 9:18-24*

A reading from the Gospel of St Luke

Jesus was praying quietly with his disciples when suddenly he asked them, 'Who do people say that I am?'

The disciples answered, 'Some believe you are John the Baptist, some say Elijah and others think that you are a prophet who has come back to life.'

'But, tell me, who do you say that I am?' asked Jesus.

Then Peter spoke, 'Master, you are the Son of God.'

Jesus told them not to tell anyone about what they had heard that day. 'It is the Son of Man's fate to suffer scorn and rejection at the hands of the Jewish leaders, before being put to death, and on the third day raised up again. Anyone who wants to follow me, must put all else aside and take up their own cross. Whoever wants to save their life will lose it, but anyone who loses their life on my behalf, will indeed save it.'

This is the Gospel of the Lord
**Praise to you, Lord Jesus Christ**

# Thirteenth Sunday of the Year

*Luke 9:51-62*

A reading from the Gospel of St Luke

Jesus set out for Jerusalem, intending to stop and rest at a Samaritan village on the way. The people there had heard that he was coming and drove Jesus and his followers away. Some of his disciples grew angry when this happened, but Jesus scolded them, and quietly led them away to another village.

As they walked, they met a man who said to Jesus, 'Lord, I am ready to follow wherever you lead.'

Jesus said to him, 'Foxes have dens and birds have nests, but the Son of God has nowhere to rest.'

Along the way Jesus invited another man to follow him, and the man replied, 'Sir, first let me bury my dead father.'

Jesus said to him, 'Leave someone else to bury the dead, for it is more important that you tell others about God's kingdom.'

Another man who was ready to follow Jesus said to him, 'First I must say goodbye to my family and friends.'

But Jesus told him, 'Anyone who begins to plough and keeps looking back is unfit for the kingdom of God.'

This is the Gospel of the Lord
**Praise to you, Lord Jesus Christ**

# Fourteenth Sunday of the Year

*Luke 10:1-12, 17-20*

A reading from the Gospel of St Luke

Jesus chose seventy-two of his disciples and sent them out in pairs, to all the places he planned to visit. 'The harvest is good but there are few workers to gather it in,' he said, 'so we must ask the Lord of the harvest to send more workers.'

Then he gave them these instructions: 'You will be like lambs among the wolves. Carry no bag or money, and stop to speak to no one on the road. Make your first words in someone's house "Peace be with you", and if a peaceful man lives in that house your peace will rest on him; otherwise it will return to you. Stay in the house where you are welcomed and share whatever food and drink they offer. Cure those who are sick and tell everyone that the kingdom of God is very near. If people are unfriendly or nasty towards you, then leave that place and wipe the dust from your feet as you go. That place will receive what it deserves at the end of time.'

Later, the seventy-two returned to Jesus filled with joy because of everything they had been able to do in his name.

Jesus told them, 'Rejoice because of the power and authority I have given to you, but even more because your names are written in heaven.'

This is the Gospel of the Lord
**Praise to you, Lord Jesus Christ**

# Fifteenth Sunday of the Year

*Luke 10:25-37*

A reading from the Gospel of St Luke.

A man stood up and asked Jesus a tricky question: 'Master, what must I do to have eternal life?'

So Jesus said to him, 'Tell me what the Scriptures say and what you think they mean.'

The man answered, 'Love God with your whole heart and soul, and with all your strength and mind,' and then he added, 'and love your neighbour as yourself.'

Jesus said to him, 'Your answer is correct, and if you do this then you will live.'

'But who is my neighbour?' the man asked.

Then Jesus told him this story:

> One day a man was travelling from Jerusalem to Jericho when a gang of robbers attacked him. They beat him up, and after stealing everything he had, they left him lying injured by the roadside. A short time later one of the Temple priests passed that way, but he crossed the road and walked on. Soon another traveller came, but he too passed by. Then a Samaritan happened to pass, and when he saw the injured man he took pity on him. He bandaged his wounds, and carried him on horseback to a nearby inn. There he cared for him and when the time came to leave, he left the innkeeper enough money to pay for the man's room until he was better.

Jesus then asked the man, 'Which man in the story was a good neighbour?'

'The one who helped the wounded traveller,' he answered.

'Go then and do the same for anyone who needs your help.'

This is the Gospel of the Lord
**Praise to you, Lord Jesus Christ**

# Sixteenth Sunday of the Year

*Luke 10:38-42*

A reading from the Gospel of St Luke

One day Jesus and his disciples came to the village called Bethany where his friends Martha and Mary lived. They welcomed Jesus and his followers and invited them to stay for a meal.

While Martha busied herself preparing and serving the food, her sister Mary sat calmly beside Jesus and listened to him talking. Martha worked hard, and all the while Mary sat listening to Jesus. Finally Martha got upset and said to Jesus, 'Lord, must I do all this work on my own? Tell Mary to come and help me!'

'Martha, Martha,' Jesus said, 'do not let these things upset you, they are not important. Mary has chosen to listen to me and that is the most important thing of all.'

This is the Gospel of the Lord
**Praise to you, Lord Jesus Christ**

## SEVENTEENTH SUNDAY OF THE YEAR

*Luke 11:1-13*

A reading from the Gospel of St Luke

When Jesus had finished praying, one of his disciples said to him, 'Master, teach us how to pray, just as John the Baptist taught his disciples.'

So Jesus said to them:
> This is what to say when you pray:

> Heavenly Father, holy is your name,
> may your kingdom come;
> each day give us our daily bread,
> and forgive our sins,
> as we forgive those who do us wrong,
> and do not put us to the test.

> Imagine a friend of yours arrives unexpectedly late at night, and you have no food to offer him, so you go to a neighbour's house to ask for some bread for your guest. Suppose he says to you, 'Go away, it is very late and I have already gone to bed,' what would happen then? If at first he will not get up even though his neighbour is standing outside his door, he will eventually get up if you persist and keep on asking!

> Anyone who asks will be answered; anyone who looks, will find, and anyone who knocks will have the door opened. If you, sinful as you are, know how to give good things to your children, then how much more will your Father in heaven give the Holy Spirit to anyone who asks him.

This is the Gospel of the Lord
**Praise to you, Lord Jesus Christ**

# Eighteenth Sunday of the Year

*Luke 12:13-21*

A reading from the Gospel of St Luke

A man in the crowd said to Jesus, 'Master, tell my brother that he must divide my father's property equally between us!'

Jesus said to him, 'My friend, who gave me the right to judge your affairs?'

Then Jesus went on to warn the people there, 'Take care not to be greedy, for having possessions and wealth will not make your life rich.'

Then he told them this parable:

> Once there was a rich man who owned many farms. One year the harvest was so good that the man could not store it all in his many barns.
>
> 'I will build bigger and better barns,' he said, 'and then I will be so rich that I will have nothing to worry about.'
>
> But God said to the man, 'You are a foolish man! When you die, what use will your worldly riches be, because in the eyes of God you are poor indeed.'

This is the Gospel of the Lord
**Praise to you, Lord Jesus Christ**

# NINETEENTH SUNDAY OF THE YEAR

*Luke 12:32-48*

A reading from the Gospel of St Luke

Jesus said to his disciples:

> You have nothing to fear, my little flock, for your heavenly Father has chosen to give you the kingdom. Sell everything you have and give the money to those who have nothing. Get yourselves purses that will not wear out, and save your treasure in heaven where it cannot be stolen or spoiled. For wherever your treasure is, your heart will be there too.
>
> Keep yourselves ready just like the servants waiting for their master to return from a wedding party. As soon as he knocks on the door, they are ready to let him in. How happy he will be to find them always prepared, however early or late he returns. Indeed, I tell you, he will sit them down and then serve them himself!
>
> If someone knows when to expect a burglar, they will be prepared and make sure that he cannot get in. You too must keep yourselves ready, because the Son of Man will return when you are least expecting him.

Peter then asked Jesus, 'Lord, is this parable meant for everyone or just for us?'

Jesus replied:

> Who is the wise servant that the master can trust to take care of his household? If the master returns to find all as it should be, he will

trust that servant to care for everything he owns. But if the master returns to find his household in confusion and disarray, because his servant did not expect him, then he will send him away and trust him no more. Those who know what their master expects from them, but choose to disregard him, will receive the appropriate punishment. If someone has been trusted with a great deal, then a great deal will be expected from that person.

This is the Gospel of the Lord
**Praise to you, Lord Jesus Christ**

## TWENTIETH SUNDAY OF THE YEAR

*Luke 12:49-53*

A reading from the Gospel of St Luke

Jesus said to them:

> I have come to set fire to the earth, and how I wish that it was already alight! I have not come to bring peace and unity, but to divide people and set them against each other; father against son, and mother against daughter.

This is the Gospel of the Lord
**Praise to you, Lord Jesus Christ**

# Twenty-first Sunday of the Year

*Luke 13:22-30*

A reading from the Gospel of St Luke

On the way to Jerusalem, someone stopped Jesus and asked, 'Master, will many be saved at the end of time?'

Jesus answered:

> Many will try to enter the kingdom of God but few will succeed. It will be no use knocking on the door which the master has already locked. However hard you protest, he will say, 'Go away, I do not know you!' And there will be weeping and wailing from those who are excluded, when they see their ancestors and God's people gathered from far and wide, feasting together in the kingdom of God. Then those who have been last will be first, and those who are first will be last.

This is the Gospel of the Lord
**Praise to you, Lord Jesus Christ**

# Twenty-second Sunday of the Year

*Luke 14:1, 7-14*

A reading from the Gospel of St Luke

One day Jesus went to the house of a Pharisee to share a Sabbath meal. Many guests had been invited and noticing how they rushed to take the best seats, Jesus said to them:

> When you are invited for a meal, do not take the best place because a more important guest might be there. You will be embarrassed when the host asks you to move and give up your seat. Instead, always sit in the least important place, so that when you are moved to a better seat others will see how much you are respected. For those who make themselves great will be humbled, and those who are humble will be made great.

> Do not invite people to eat with you because you know they can invite you back. Be generous and invite those who cannot repay your kindness. You will be rewarded for your goodness at the end of time.

This is the Gospel of the Lord
**Praise to you, Lord Jesus Christ**

# Twenty-third Sunday of the Year

*Luke 14:25-33*

A reading from the Gospel of St Luke

A crowd of people were following Jesus, and he said to them:

> If you want to be one of my disciples you must be ready to love me more than your own family and even yourself. If you do not carry your own cross and come with me, then you cannot be my disciple.
>
> If a man plans to build a house, he works out how much it will cost before he begins. Otherwise he might lay the foundations and then find that he cannot afford to finish the work. If a king's army of ten thousand men was preparing to fight an army of twenty thousand men, would the king not consider whether he might win or lose? If defeat was likely, then he would send out messengers to make peace with his enemy.
>
> If anyone plans to follow me, he must count the cost of giving up everything to be my disciple.

This is the Gospel of the Lord
**Praise to you, Lord Jesus Christ**

# Twenty-fourth Sunday of the Year

*Luke 15:1-32*

A reading from the Gospel of St Luke

The Pharisees and scribes complained about Jesus spending so much time with the tax collectors and sinners. When he heard this, he told these parables:

> If a shepherd with a hundred sheep discovered that one of those sheep had strayed from the flock and got lost, would he not leave the ninety-nine and search for the last one until he found it? Then he would carry it home, rejoicing, and call all his friends to celebrate with him and share his delight. In the same way, I tell you, there will be more rejoicing in heaven over one sinner who repents than over ninety-nine good people who have nothing to be sorry for.

> Or suppose a woman had ten drachmas, and found that one of her precious coins was missing. Surely she would take a lamp and sweep the house from top to bottom, searching everywhere until she found that coin. Then she would call her friends to share her happiness at finding what she had lost. In the same way, God's angels rejoice and celebrate over one person who is sorry for their sins.

Then Jesus told them another parable:

> There was a man who had two sons and the younger one came to his father and said, 'Father, give me everything that will one day belong to me, so I can enjoy my riches now.'

> The father did this, and the son set off to look

for adventure. He travelled to a distant land and spent all his money enjoying himself.

There was a famine in that land, and the young man found himself penniless and hungry. 'If I stay here I will surely starve,' he thought, so he decided to return to his father and ask for his forgiveness.

The father saw his son coming and ran to welcome him. As he hugged him, the young man said, 'Father, I am so sorry. I no longer deserve to be called your son.'

But the father told his servants to prepare a feast and to bring the finest clothes, and they began to celebrate.

When the man's other son returned home from working in the fields, he asked the servants, 'What is the reason for such a celebration?'

When he heard their explanation, he was filled with anger and refused to join the party. So his father came looking for him and the son said to him, 'I have been hard-working and loyal, and never once did you throw such a party for me. Yet you are happy to do so for my brother who has been greedy and selfish and treated you very badly.'

The father answered his son, 'You are always with me, and everything I have belongs to you. You brother who was lost, has been found. He is not dead after all, but alive, and it is only right that we should celebrate his return with joy!'

This is the Gospel of the Lord
**Praise to you, Lord Jesus Christ**

# TWENTY-FIFTH SUNDAY OF THE YEAR

*Luke 16:1-13*

A reading from the Gospel of St Luke

Jesus told his disciples a parable:

A rich man, who had a servant to manage his affairs, sent for him one day. 'I have heard that you are wasting my money,' he said, 'so I want to see your accounts, and dismiss you from your job.'

The servant was dismayed, 'What am I to do now?' he wondered. 'I am not strong enough for manual work, and I don't want to beg!'

Then he had an idea! One by one he sent for everyone who owed his master money, to settle their debts. 'How much do you owe my master?' he asked the first.

'One hundred jars of oil,' came the reply.

'Here is your account,' he said. 'Quickly, write down fifty and I will be satisfied.'

As each debtor came to settle their account, the servant accepted less than they owed. 'When I am dismissed,' he thought, 'they will remember what I have done for them, and treat me kindly.'

When his master heard what the dishonest servant had been doing, he praised him for his shrewdness, because the worldly wise are more astute in dealing with their own kind than are people of the light.

Then Jesus said:

When a person is honest about the small

things in life, then they will be honest about more important things too. If you cannot be trusted with something as unimportant as money, how can you be trusted with the most precious treasure of all? No one can be the servant of two masters, and you cannot serve both God and money.

This is the Gospel of the Lord
**Praise to you, Lord Jesus Christ**

HEAR THE GOOD NEWS

# TWENTY-SIXTH SUNDAY OF THE YEAR

*Luke 16:19-31*

A reading from the Gospel of St Luke

One day Jesus told this story:

Once there was a rich man who had fine clothes and the best of everything that money could buy. He spent his time enjoying himself and feasting with his rich friends.

On the street outside his house lay a poor man called Lazarus who was thin and hungry, and covered in sores. Lazarus would gladly have eaten the rich man's scraps, if they had been offered to him. Lazarus died and went to heaven where Abraham took care of him, and he was truly happy at last.

When the rich man died he went to hell, and seeing Lazarus so happy, he cried out to Abraham for help.

Abraham said to him, 'You enjoyed a life of luxury and comfort, while Lazarus suffered. Now Lazarus is being consoled while it is your turn to suffer. It is too late to change things now.'

So the rich man begged Abraham to send someone from the dead to warn his brothers of what suffering awaited them unless they changed their ways.

Abraham said to him, 'They already know what to do! If they will not listen to Moses and the prophets, then even someone from the grave will not convince them!'

This is the Gospel of the Lord
**Praise to you, Lord Jesus Chris**

# Twenty-seventh Sunday of the Year

*Luke 17:5-10*

A reading from the Gospel of St Luke

One day the apostles said to Jesus, 'Master make our faith grow.'

Jesus told them:

> With just a little faith you can do marvellous things. If your faith was the size of a mustard seed, you could command this mulberry tree to uproot and plant itself in the sea, and it would do what you said!

Then Jesus said to them:

> Imagine you had a servant and you gave him orders to plough your field. When he had finished and returned from work, would you as his master tell him to sit down and enjoy his meal? Surely you would say, 'Get my dinner ready, and attend to my needs before you eat yourself!' The servant has only done what he was ordered to do, so should he expect any more?

> As for you, when you have done everything you have been told to do, tell yourselves, 'We have done our duty, and should expect nothing more because we are servants.'

This is the Gospel of the Lord
**Praise to you, Lord Jesus Christ**

# Twenty-eighth Sunday of the Year

*Luke 17:11-19*

A reading from the Gospel of St Luke

On the way to Jerusalem, Jesus drew near a village where he found ten lepers waiting to meet him. Keeping their distance, they called out to him, 'Jesus of Nazareth, have pity and help us!'

Jesus saw their suffering and said, 'Go and show yourselves to the priest.'

They set off to see the priest and on the way they realised that their leprosy had disappeared and they were cured!

As the others ran to find the priest, one of the ten went back to find Jesus. He threw himself down before him, praising God and thanking Jesus for his kindness.

'Were the others not cured too?' Jesus asked. 'Yet only one has bothered to thank God for his goodness.' Then he said to the man, 'Now go and see the priest, your faith in God has made you well.'

This is the Gospel of the Lord
**Praise to you, Lord Jesus Christ**

# TWENTY-NINTH SUNDAY OF THE YEAR

*Luke 18:1-8*

A reading from the Gospel of St Luke

Jesus told the people a parable to show them that they should keep on praying and never lose hope:

In a certain town there was a judge who was often unjust and unfair. A woman in the town asked the judge to help her settle a quarrel with her neighbour. The judge was not interested in the woman's problem and sent her away.

But the woman did not give up! She came back every day, day in and day out, until the judge could not stand being pestered any more.

'I must give this woman what she wants,' he said, 'or she will never give me any peace.'

Then Jesus said: 'If such a man can finally listen and do what is asked of him, how much more will my heavenly Father do for you if you keep on asking.'

This is the Gospel of the Lord
**Praise to you, Lord Jesus Christ**

## THIRTIETH SUNDAY OF THE YEAR

*Luke 18:9-14*

A reading from the Gospel of St Luke

Jesus told a parable aimed at people who were certain of their own goodness, and looked down on everyone else:

> Two men went to the Temple to pray. One was a Pharisee, an upright and religious man who always obeyed the law. The other was a tax collector who cheated people to make himself rich.
>
> The Pharisee stood up and prayed, 'Thank you, God, for making me such a good person, unlike the tax collector over there! I keep all your rules and am most generous with my money.'
>
> The tax collector stood at the back of the Temple. He bowed his head in shame as he prayed quietly, 'O God, I have done so many things wrong. Please forgive me.'

Jesus said, 'It was the second man, and not the first, who pleased God with his prayer. For anyone who makes themselves important will be brought low, and any who is humble will be raised high.'

This is the Gospel of the Lord
**Praise to you, Lord Jesus Christ**

# Thirty-first Sunday of the Year

*Luke 19:1-10*

A reading from the Gospel of St Luke

Jesus went to a town called Jericho, where a man called Zacchaeus lived. Nobody liked Zacchaeus because he was a tax collector who cheated people to make himself rich.

When Jesus arrived, crowds gathered to see him and Zacchaeus was among them. Zacchaeus was very small and could not see Jesus because of the crowds, so he climbed a tree to get a better view. As Jesus passed by, he looked up and said, 'Come down, Zacchaeus! I want to visit your house today.'

Zacchaeus almost fell out of the tree with surprise. Hearing this, the crowd began to grumble and complain. 'How can Jesus speak to such a wicked man!' they said.

Then Zacchaeus turned to Jesus. 'Lord,' he said, 'I know that I am a dishonest cheat, but I want to change and put things right! I will give half of everything I own to the poor, and pay back everything I have stolen four times over.'

Jesus smiled at Zacchaeus and said, 'I have come to find and save anyone who has lost their way. Now change your heart and make a fresh start.'

This is the Gospel of the Lord
**Praise to you, Lord Jesus Christ**

# THIRTY-SECOND SUNDAY OF THE YEAR

*Luke 20:27-38*

A reading from the Gospel of St Luke

The Sadducees (who did not believe in life after death) put this question to Jesus: 'If a woman's husband dies, and she marries his brother who also dies, which man will be her husband when she is dead and they all meet again in the next life?'

Jesus answered them, 'In this life they may have been husband and wife, but in the next life they will all be children of God. After the resurrection from the dead, those who are chosen will never die again, and they will share everlasting life and happiness together with the angels in heaven. Moses himself showed us in the story of the burning bush that the dead are raised to life. Did he not call the Lord the God of Abraham, Isaac and Jacob? He is God of the living not the dead, and for him everyone is alive.'

This is the Gospel of the Lord
**Praise to you, Lord Jesus Christ**

# THIRTY-THIRD SUNDAY OF THE YEAR

*Luke 21:5-19*

A reading from the Gospel of St Luke

Some of the a crowd were discussing how grand and beautiful the Temple in Jerusalem was. Jesus said to them, 'A time will come when all this will be destroyed.'

'Master, when will this happen?' they asked. 'What warning will there be?'

Jesus told them:

> Take care not to be misled by those who come and claim to speak for me. Many things will happen before the end, so do not panic. There will be wars and fighting; earthquakes and disasters; famines and plagues and signs in the heavens. Before then many will suffer because they are my followers. I will give them courage and strength, and words of wisdom, and they will be rewarded for their faith and goodness by my heavenly Father.

This is the Gospel of the Lord
**Praise to you, Lord Jesus Christ**

# CHRIST THE KING

*Luke 23:35-43*

A reading from the Gospel of St Luke

As the crowd stood watching, their leaders derided Jesus, saying, 'If he is so great, if he is the chosen one of God, then why doesn't he save himself like he saved others?'

Even the soldiers made fun of him and they hung a sign above him which read, 'This is the King of the Jews'.

One of the criminals hanging next to Jesus jeered at him, 'Call yourself a Messiah! If you were, you could save yourself and us as well!'

But the other criminal answered sharply, 'Leave him alone! We deserve to be punished but he has done nothing wrong.' Then he said to Jesus, 'Do not forget me in your kingdom.'

Jesus answered him, 'Today you will be with me in paradise.'

This is the Gospel of the Lord
**Praise to you, Lord Jesus Christ**

# SPECIAL FEASTS
Years A, B and C

# Mary, Mother of God – 1 January

*Luke 2:16-21*

A reading from the Gospel of St Luke

The shepherds hurried to Bethlehem and found the place where the baby lay in a manger, watched over by Mary and Joseph. The shepherds told them what they had seen and heard that night, and Mary and Joseph shared their wonder. Mary listened carefully and cherished all these things in her heart.

Then the shepherds went back to their flocks on the hillside, singing God's praises because everything had been as the angel had said.

When the time came for the child to be circumcised on the eighth day, they named him Jesus, just as the angel had told them.

This is the Gospel of the Lord
**Praise to you, Lord Jesus Christ**

# The Annunciation of the Lord – 25 March

*Luke 1:26-38*

A reading from the Gospel of St Luke

God sent the angel Gabriel to a town in Galilee called Nazareth, to a young woman there called Mary. She was engaged to marry a carpenter called Joseph, a descendant of King David's family.

The angel greeted Mary with the words, 'Be glad, Mary, for God is with you and has given you great blessings.'

Mary was troubled and wondered what the angel's words meant.

'There is nothing to fear,' Gabriel assured her. 'You will have a son and name him Jesus. He will be called Son of the Most High, whose reign will never end.'

'How can this happen,' asked Mary, 'when I am not married?'

'The Holy Spirit will come to you,' said Gabriel. 'Therefore this child will be holy and be known as the Son of God. Nothing is impossible for God. Your cousin Elizabeth who was childless, is herself expecting a baby.'

Then Mary said, 'I am God's servant, and will do whatever he asks. Let everything happen just as you have said.'

Then the angel left her.

This is the Gospel of the Lord
**Praise to you, Lord Jesus Christ**

# THE PRESENTATION OF THE LORD – 2 FEBRUARY

*Luke 2:22-40*

A reading from the Gospel of St Luke

Mary and Joseph took Jesus to the Temple to present him to the Lord, and to offer sacrifice as required by the law of Moses. (Every first-born boy must be dedicated to God and a sacrifice of two turtledoves or a pair of young pigeons must be offered).

Living in Jerusalem was a man called Simeon who was filled with the Holy Spirit and had been promised by God that he would not die until he had seen the Christ. The Spirit guided Simeon to the Temple that day and when he set eyes on Jesus, he took the child in his arms and began to praise God and give him thanks: 'Now Lord, let me die in peace. Just as you promised, I have seen the Saviour you have sent to reveal your love and glory, not just for your people Israel but for everyone.'

Mary and Joseph were full of wonder at everything being said about Jesus. Simeon blessed them both, and turning to Mary he said, 'He will cause many in Israel to fall and many to rise, he will be rejected and scorned, and your own heart will be pierced by a terrible sword.'

Anna, the daughter of Phanuel, was an elderly prophetess who lived in the Temple. She spent her life serving God through constant prayer and fasting. As soon as she saw Jesus, Anna began to praise God and tell everyone about the child who would save Jerusalem.

When Mary and Joseph had done everything that the law required, they took Jesus home to Nazareth in Galilee. There he grew into a strong and wise young man, and he was blessed by God.

This is the Gospel of the Lord
**Praise to you, Lord Jesus Christ**

# Saint John the Baptist – 24 June

*Luke 1:57-66, 80*

A reading from the Gospel of St Luke

When her time came, Elizabeth the wife of Zechariah gave birth to a son. Their friends and family joyfully celebrated God's great kindness and blessing, for Elizabeth and her husband were both elderly.

When the child was eight days old it was time for him to be circumcised and given a name. Everyone assumed that he would be called Zechariah after his father, but Elizabeth declared, 'His name will be John'.

Since no one in the child's family went by this name, the people turned to Zechariah for his opinion in the matter. Zechariah, who remained struck dumb, had to write the reply: 'His name is John!' At that very moment his speech returned, and he began to give glory and praise to God.

Throughout the countryside of Judaea people discussed these marvellous events and pondered what the future held for this remarkable child.

God's favour rested on John and he grew strong in body and spirit. He went to live in the desert until the time came for him to begin preaching to the people.

This is the Gospel of the Lord
**Praise to you, Lord Jesus Christ**

## SAINTS PETER AND PAUL – 29 JUNE

*Matthew 16:13-19*

A reading from the Gospel of St Matthew

One day Jesus asked his disciples, 'Who do people say that I am?'

'Some people say that you are John the Baptist; others say that you are Elijah or Jeremiah or one of the other wise prophets from the past.'

Then Jesus said, 'But who do you say that I am?'

The disciples were silent until Peter said, 'You are the Christ, the Son of the living God.'

Jesus smiled at Peter and said, 'My heavenly Father has helped you to understand this. You are Peter (Petros), and on this rock (Petra) I will build my Church. I will give you the keys to the kingdom of heaven; whatever you enforce here on earth will be enforced in heaven, whatever you dismiss here on earth will be dismissed in heaven.'

This is the Gospel of the Lord
**Praise to you, Lord Jesus Christ**

# THE TRANSFIGURATION OF THE LORD – 6 AUGUST

*Year A – Matthew 17:1-9*

A reading from the Gospel of St Matthew

One day Jesus asked Peter, James and John to come and pray with him. He led them to the top of a steep mountain, where it was peaceful and quiet, and where they could be alone.

Jesus began to pray to his heavenly Father and suddenly he appeared to change! His face and clothes shone with a brilliant light, as dazzling as the rays of the sun.

Then the disciples saw Moses and Elijah on either side of Jesus, talking to him. Peter jumped up with excitement and said, 'Lord, this is wonderful! I could make three shelters – one for each of you!'

At that moment a cloud streaming with light appeared above them, and a voice said, 'This is my Son, whom I love very much. Listen to what he says.'

The disciples were so terrified that they threw themselves to the ground and hid their faces.

Then Jesus said gently, 'Get up, my friends, do not be afraid.'

When they looked up, Jesus was standing alone. As they came down the mountain together, Jesus told them firmly, 'You must not tell anyone about what you have seen today, until the Son of Man has risen from the dead.'

This is the Gospel of the Lord
**Praise to you, Lord Jesus Christ**

# THE TRANSFIGURATION OF THE LORD – 6 AUGUST

*Year B – Mark 9:2-10*

A reading from the Gospel of St Mark

Jesus led Peter, James and John to the top of a high mountain where they could be alone. While they looked on, Jesus' appearance was transformed as his clothes shone brilliantly white. Then Elijah and Moses appeared before them and began talking to Jesus.

The disciples were so afraid they did not know what to do or say, until Peter spoke up. 'Master, it is wonderful for us to be here. We could make a shelter for each one of you!'

At that moment a passing cloud covered them with its shadow, and a voice came from the cloud and said, 'This is my Son whom I love very much. Listen to what he says.'

Then suddenly they found themselves alone with Jesus, who told them not to tell anyone what they had seen until the Son of Man had risen from the dead. They did what Jesus asked, but discussed amongst themselves what 'rising from the dead' could possibly mean.

This is the Gospel of the Lord
**Praise to you, Lord Jesus Christ**

# THE TRANSFIGURATION OF THE LORD – 6 AUGUST

*Year C – Luke 9:28-36*

A reading from the Gospel of St Luke

With the disciples Peter, James and John, Jesus climbed a mountain to pray. While Jesus prayed, his clothes shone with dazzling white light as radiant as the sun, and his appearance was transformed!

Suddenly, Moses and Elijah appeared in glory next to Jesus and began speaking to him.

Peter and his friends were amazed by everything they saw, and Peter said to Jesus, 'Lord, this is all so wonderful! I could build three shelters, one for each of you!'

At that moment a cloud descended and covered them on the mountain top, and the disciples were afraid. Then a voice from the cloud spoke, 'This is my Son, the chosen one, listen to what he says.'

When the voice fell silent, the disciples found themselves alone with Jesus. The three friends told no one at that time about the wonders they had witnessed that day.

This is the Gospel of the Lord
**Praise to you, Lord Jesus Christ**

# THE ASSUMPTION OF THE BLESSED VIRGIN MARY – 15 AUGUST

*Luke 1:39-56*

A reading from the Gospel of St Luke

After the angel Gabriel had appeared to Mary she set off at once to visit her cousin Elizabeth. When Elizabeth saw Mary coming she ran to welcome her, and the baby inside her leapt for joy at the sound of Mary's greeting.

Elizabeth was filled with the Holy Spirit and said to Mary, 'Of all women you are the most blessed, and blessed is your unborn child, because you believed in the power of God and he has chosen you to be the mother of my Lord.'

And Mary said:
> My soul praises God,
> and my spirit is filled with joy in God my saviour.
> The Lord has looked kindly on his lowly servant.
> Now and for evermore all people will call me blessed.
> Almighty God has done great things for me;
> holy is his name.
> All who worship him
> know God's unending love.
> With his strong arm
> God overthrows the proud;
> he humbles kings
> and raises the meek high.
> God satisfies the starving with good things
> but to the rich he gives nothing.
> God protects his people Israel,

and remembers his promise of mercy
to Abraham and his descendants for all time.

Mary stayed with her cousin Elizabeth for three months before returning home.

This is the Gospel of the Lord
**Praise to you, Lord Jesus Christ**

# THE TRIUMPH OF THE HOLY CROSS – 14 SEPTEMBER

*John 3:13-17*

A reading from the Gospel of St John

Jesus said to Nicodemus:

> Only the Son of Man has been in heaven and returned from there. Just as Moses raised up the snake in the desert, so too must the Son of Man be raised up, so that those who believe in him may have eternal life.
>
> Because God loved the world so much, he sent his only Son to be its Saviour and not its judge, and to rescue from death all who believe in him.

This is the Gospel of the Lord
**Praise to you, Lord Jesus Christ**

# All Saints – 1 November

*Matthew 5:1-12*

A reading from the Gospel of St Matthew

A crowd of disciples gathered around, and Jesus sat down and began to preach to them:

Happy are the poor in spirit, for the kingdom of heaven is theirs.

Happy are the broken-hearted, for they will be comforted.

Happy are the meek and gentle, for the earth will belong to them.

Happy are those who hunger and thirst for what is right, for justice will be theirs.

Happy are those who show forgiveness, because they will receive forgiveness in return.

Happy are those with a pure heart, for they shall see the face of God.

Happy are the peace-makers; God will call them his children.

Happy are those who suffer because they stand up for what is right; the kingdom of heaven belongs to them.

Be happy when people harass and mistreat you, and tell lies about you because you are my disciples. All this was suffered by the prophets who came before you. Be glad because when the time comes you will be richly rewarded in heaven.

This is the Gospel of the Lord
**Praise to you, Lord Jesus Christ**

# FEASTS OF THE DEDICATION OF A CHURCH

*John 4:19-24*

A reading from the Gospel of St John

The Samaritan woman said to Jesus, 'Sir, I can see that you are a prophet from God. You must know that since our ancestors' time we have worshipped here on Mount Gerizim, instead of the Temple in Jerusalem as the Jews do.'

Jesus said to the woman, 'The time is coming when you will worship God neither here nor in Jerusalem. Unlike you, the Jewish people know whom they worship, and that he is the God of salvation. What is important to God is that you worship him in spirit and truth.'

This is the Gospel of the Lord
**Praise to you, Lord Jesus Christ**

# PRONUNCIATION GUIDE

This is an extract from the comprehensive guide in Margaret Rizza's helpful book *Proclaiming God's Word – a handbook for readers* (Kevin Mayhew, 1998). It does not claim to be infallible. It is provided simply to help the reader with some general guidelines on pronunciation of the names of people and places in the Bible. These biblical names have been written phonetically, each syllable and vowel being given separately with its appropriate stress.

A brief explanation of the vowel sounds is given below, followed by a table of names with the syllable on which the stress falls printed in bold capital letters.

**Vowels**

Aa
- long a, (a) as in 'may', e.g. Abraham
- short a, (a) as in 'bat', e.g. Arimathaea
- final a is pronounced 'ah', e.g. Cana
- ae is pronounced e, as in 'fee', e.g. Caesar
- ai is pronounced i, as in 'bite', e.g. Jairus, Isaiah
- ar is pronounced ah, as in final a, as in 'car', e.g. Bartimaeus
- au is pronounced aw, as in 'law', e.g. Augustus

Ee
- long e, (e) as in 'fee', e.g. Cephas
- short e, (e) as in 'get', e.g. Elisha

### Ii
- long i, (i̱) pronounced 'eye' as in 'site', e.g. Isaiah
- short i, (i) as in 'fit', e.g. Simeon
- final i is long, e.g. Philippi

### Oo
- long o, (o̱) as in 'dote', e.g. Noah
- short o, (o) as in 'hot', e.g. Golgotha

### Uu
- short u, (u) oo as in 'soot', but occasionally 'ew', e.g. Emmanuel, Sadducees

### Yy
- y as long i, as in 'why', e.g. Cyrene
- y as short i, as in 'jelly', e.g. Bethany

## Consonants

### Cc
- as in English, hard before a, o and u, as in 'cap', 'cog', and 'cub', e.g. Cain, Colossus
- hard before consonants, e.g. Cleopas
- soft before e and i, as in 'ceiling', 'cipher', e.g. Cephas, Cilicia
- soft before ae and y, e.g. Caesarea, Cyrene.

## Stress

In order to indicate where the stress or accent falls in a name, the accented syllable is printed in bold capitals, for example, E-**MA**-nu-el.

# PRONUNCIATION GUIDE

### Double vowels and consonants

To simplify further the phonetic pronunciation, where there are double consonants and vowels the one which would be mute anyway has been omitted.

| | |
|---|---|
| Abraham | **A**-bra-ham |
| Alphaeus | al-**PHAE**-us |
| Arimathaea | a-ri-ma-**THAE**-a |
| Augustus | au-**GUS**-tus |
| | |
| Barabbas | ba-**RA**-bas |
| Bartimaeus | bar-ti-**MAE**-us |
| Bethany | **BE**-tha-ny |
| Bethphage | **BETH**-pha-ge |
| | |
| Caesar | **CAE**-sar |
| Caesarea | cae-sa-**RE**-a |
| C. Philippi | C. **PHI**-li-pi |
| Caiaphas | **CA**-i-a-phas |
| Cana | **CA**-na |
| Canaanite | **CA**-na-nite |
| Capernaum | ca-**PER**-na-um |
| Cephas | **CE**-phas |
| Cleophas | **CLE**-o-phas |
| Cyrene | cy-**RE**-ne |
| | |
| Elijah | e **LI** jah |
| Elisha | e-**LI**-sha |
| Emmanuel | e-**MA**-nu-el |
| Emmaus | e-**MA**-us |
| | |
| Galilean | ga-li-**LE**-an |
| Gerizim | ge-ri-**ZIM** |
| Gethsemane | geth-**SE**-ma-ne |
| Golgotha | **GOL**-go-tha |

| | |
|---|---|
| Isaiah | i-SA-i-ah |
| Iscariot | is-CA-ri-ot |
| | |
| Jairus | JAI-rus |
| Jeremiah | je-re-MI-ah |
| Jericho | JE-ri-cho |
| Judaea | ju-DAE-a |
| Judaean | ju-DAE-an |
| | |
| Lazarus | LA-za-rus |
| | |
| Magdala | MAG-da-la |
| Messiah | me-SI-ah |
| | |
| Naaman | NA-man |
| Nain | NA-in |
| Nazareth | NA-za-reth |
| Nicodemus | ni-co-DE-mus |
| Noah | NO-ah |
| | |
| Phanuel | PHA-nu-el |
| Pharisees | PHA-ri-ses |
| Pontius Pilate | PON-tius PI-late |
| | |
| Rabbi | RA-bi |
| | |
| Sadducees | SAD-u-ces |
| Salome | sa-LO-me |
| Samaritans | sa-MA-ri-tans |
| Sanhedrin | san-HE-drin |
| Sidon | SI-don |
| Siloam | si-LO-am |
| Simeon | SI-me-on |
| Sychar | SY-char |
| | |
| Thaddaeus | tha-DAE-us |

| | |
|---|---|
| Tiberius | ti-**BE**-ri-us |
| Tyre | **TYRE** |
| | |
| Zacchaeus | za-**CHAE**-us |
| Zebedee | **ZE**-be-de |
| Zechariah | ze-cha-**RI**-ah |
| Zion | **ZI**-on |